DELIVERANCE
FROM
Oppression

LINDY LANE

Copyright © 2016 by Lindy Lane

Deliverance from Oppression
by Lindy Lane

Printed in the United States of America.

ISBN 9781498465458

All rights reserved solely by the author. The author guarantees all contents are original and do not infringe upon the legal rights of any other person or work. No part of this book may be reproduced in any form without the permission of the author. The views expressed in this book are not necessarily those of the publisher.

Unless otherwise indicated, Scripture quotations taken from the King James Version (KJV) – *public domain.*

www.xulonpress.com

DEDICATION:

To Carol and Margo, a source of courage; my support team;
You have given me fortitude to endure.
To my son for holding me up and cheering me on,
so I can keep going.
Thank you

FOREWORD

When I first met Lindy it was all about a small herd of wild horses in the mountains that surround my home. She was as taken by these beautiful creatures as I have been. I learned later that in most of her life she had had a horse but was currently without one. Lindy was drawn to these wild horses to fill that gap. She spent time watching them at the creek getting water and wishing she could take a few of them home with her. It was a year later Lindy drove up to my yard, where the horses were hanging out, to visit with all of us. I knew right then and there that Lindy was someone that would definitely make my life fuller and help this herd in some way; I didn't know how at that point, but I knew there was a reason she came into my life.

The story of these horses has been one traumatic event after another: from rustling attempts to being chased by people with dollar signs in their eyes for either dog food or sale of colts. After many trials and tribulations Lindy actually rescued three of these gorgeous young horses which otherwise, would have been killed or cast out of the herd, and left to fend for themselves facing starvation. I knew she was someone who could teach me a lot. She has become an amazing friend. I hope you can learn from her like I have.

Carol Shirley

TABLE OF CONTENTS

Prologue	xi
Introduction	xiii
1. My Childhood	15
2. Heroin	19
3. Busted	26
4. Abandoned	31
5. My first Son	34
6. I had a Plan	37
7. Stuffing the Gunnysacks	41
8. Serenity Shattered	44
9. Over the Mountain	48
10. Building our Lodge	55
11. Our son was Born	61
12. Always Waiting	68
13. We bought a Cow	72
14. I left the Mountain	74
15. Born Again	78
16. My new Faith	83
17. Finding the Mennonites	93
18. My Cross	101
19. Cancer	105

20. Did he Repent?	110
21. Hepatitis	116
22. The healing Prayer	119
23. Going Down to the Dunghill	125
24. The last Revival	136
25. Find a Doctor	149
26. False Teaching	152
27. Who is the Messiah?	163
28. Get Help	172
29. He loves even the Sparrows	177
30. We can Overcome	183
31. The Painting	187
Epilogue	189

PROLOGUE

This story I am about to tell you is like telling the story of someone else's life. When I became a Christian I left behind my life of sin, yet the marks of that life are engraved in my body, soul and spirit. Today I still suffer the consequences of living that life exposed to trauma, terror and oppression. I hope to only encourage others to take the hand of the One who can save you from such things as I went through over the years of my life. I often feel sorrow in my gut to think of all the wasted years living a life of self destruction, but then somehow I think there is a purpose in all things. Perhaps I have lived to write this book; to lend a helping hand to others. It is my earnest prayer to accomplish this very thing. Believe me, it has been scary to unveil my life to the whole world, but my Lord has encouraged me every step of the way. He began by giving me the vision of the Trumpeter Swans and the unfolding of the vision in this message that is portrayed in every aspect of the painting. It was a few years after the vision that I began to paint after having put away my art work for twenty-two years while I was in the Mennonite church. It took me about eight months to complete it. The Lord had His hand in it; I could not have persevered without Him. My prayer is that you, the reader, can benefit through my suffering, for even one soul delivered is worth it all.

Introduction

Webster's 1828 Dictionary [K-Z]

oppression

OPPRES'SION, n.
1. The act of oppressing; the imposition of unreasonable burdens, either in taxes or services; cruelty; severity.
2. The state of being oppressed or overburdened; misery. The Lord– saw the oppression of Israel. II Kings. 8.
3. Hardship; calamity.
4. Depression; dullness of spirits; lassitude of body.
5. A sense of heaviness or weight in the breast, &c.

I would like to talk to you about my experience and lift out suggestions that I wish someone had told me when I was in the midst of this awful imprisonment of oppression. I am not a psychologist or a doctor, nevertheless I hope that my experiences can give insight and hope to anyone who may be caught in the prison of oppression. Perhaps for you, it could be a number of other situations that have you trapped. But there is hope and there is a way of escape. Seek the Way and you shall find it.

I will give fictitious names to the characters, as I do not want to harm anyone. My purpose is only to see the captives set free. You will come across words that are seemingly misspelled and sentences that are constructed oddly, as the author is attempting to present actual language as she speaks it, in real life.

I hope this book will be a source of inspiration to you and that you will find the source of strength to become an over comer, to find deliverance from the oppression in your life, whatever it may be that holds you in captivity. Never lose hope; fore it is what will keep you in the hour of despair. Remember that there is One that loves you forever.

1.

MY CHILDHOOD

A gentle breeze blew the branches of the tree top of which served as my hiding place from all insult and pain. There I sat quietly, even silently; waiting to see a little bird that might happen to come so close I could touch him. The wind bathed my weary head and cleared my mind of the confusion of so much yelling and accusing and hateful words, swaying me back and forth gently as a mother rocks her baby. I picked a hickory bud and peeled off the petals one by one. They were so silky and my fingers stroked the silk as if it were my mind, peeling away the layers of damage until I reached the inner most core, untouched by human pain. I was only a child and in my mind there was no explanation or place of refuge. I could not create a solution. My home was complete with my mama and daddy, three sisters and a brother who was long grown up and always away at college or working in a town far from home. Maybe because he was big he was able to create his place of escape. But I could not, except in the top of my tree, where no one else could climb, or in the middle of a daisy field where I would lay down in the tall grasses where no one could see me, and look up into the sky and talk to God about love. I plucked the petals off of a choice daisy as I recited, "He loves me; he loves me not; he loves me; he loves me not". My heart soared with hope if it portrayed that he loved me. But it did not always land that way and my sadness just deepened. I always wanted to have someone love me, in a tender way, like my dog or my cat did, even my lizard that I named Lazy Liza Lizard. I could hold her on my finger and pet the top of her head with my thumb, and she would lie perfectly still in my hand and fall asleep while I petted her head.

My refuge was only for a little piece of time, and then I had to return to my home and family where yelling was the way we talked to each other. There was no praise or touch; love was perhaps there in a language of service, at least through my parents. I think my sisters were bitter at the roll they were called to perform. I was the second to the youngest and my little sister and I did not have to work as hard as my two older sisters. But even at an early age we all had jobs to do. We grew a very large garden, put up food; and we all helped. There is nothing wrong with hard and consistent work; it was the yelling and screaming that went along with it that made our lives a bitter pill.

Nevertheless there were many things I am thankful for and that is that we were always a family. We did fun things together like go swimming in the Bison River in the summer time, or took a vacation to see aunts and uncles. Some lived near the ocean so we swam and these were always good memories. We saw the sights in America, and as we put on the miles, with all six of us in the car, we sang songs and enjoyed seeing all the country we passed through. But I remember the lonely feeling, looking out the window, wishing that I could take off on a horse across the expanse with the man I loved next to me. But anyway, I was just a child and there was no one who loved me.

One thing I am so glad for, that many people and families neglect to do today, to the detriment of the forming of their children's stability, is the family always sat together at the table for meals. Daddy always came home at the same time every day and brought home milk and bread. My dad was a different person than my mother. He was gentle most of the time and he too needed a refuge, and found it in tuning out everything around him. Mother had a hard time getting his attention. We always thought he was hard of hearing. Maybe he was and maybe he wasn't, but he was very successful in retreating into another world in the midst of total chaos.

My mother was the yeller and we all followed suit; it was our way of life. Now that I am grown and know a little about my mothers' past; it is no doubt that her growing up years was very hard. Her father was an alcoholic and eventually committed suicide. My grandmother then fell to mental illness. My mother quit school at an early age to work in the woolen mills. They lived in Rhode Island where winters are cold. I can only imagine that their home and work conditions were very cold. This alone causes such an unsettled feeling in our soul. My mother never talked about her feelings, nor did she talk to us children about our feelings. There was no touch except if we were slapped across our shoulder. That was all she did, so we were never physically hurt; only emotionally.

I am also thankful that mother insisted that we go to church every Sunday. Even when we traveled we looked for a motel in a town that had a Catholic church. It provided for me the belief in God the Father, God the Son and God the Holy Ghost. This I never lost even when I lived amongst the hippies. I always prayed to the Father, Son and Holy Ghost. I think this was largely how God was able to save me many years later. When I was but thirteen I rebelled against my parents and their church and refused to attend any longer. I never felt love there and never felt the presence of God; it was all dead rituals. This did not keep me contented nor offer a refuge from my turmoil. There are many strange spirits that attend to these rituals and it was some years to come before I feared those spirits and actually recognized them and sought the true God until I found Him.

2.

HEROIN

I grew to hate my parents, especially my mother. And by the time I was a teenager I wanted to leave my home, I did run away several times. I was looking for love in a man, but only found those who lied and used me, until finally when I had run away and was living in a small hut in the woods near my high school, a man named Jim, who had heard of me sought me out. He was fresh out of the Viet Nam war, and married. He wooed me and soon we fell "in love". I was sixteen; he was eight years older than I. Even though he told me it was I whom he loved, he always returned to his wife and children on a daily basis. This was very damaging to my soul and spirit, in ways that I would only understand in the years ahead; many years ahead. In spite of the nature of our relationship it grew deeper and more and more damaging. Because of his war experience he was addicted to heroin, which was easy to get in 'Nam. They used it freely on their marijuana cigarettes. This was all in the attempt to escape the horrors of war which surrounded them. The soldiers had to machine gun down women and children because they likely were carrying hand grenades. Along the roads through the jungles that they drove their tanks on were the body parts strewn from previous massacres. These men were barely more than boys, forced into this murderous war. Drugs were their only escape.

Jim requested medical discharge for his heroin addiction and it was granted him. But he received no medical treatment to overcome the addiction; he had a dishonorable discharge with no benefits.

One day he came to me at my hut in the woods and wanted me to go with him to the city where he knew some friends. I had to skip school, in which I was half-heartedly trying to maintain attendance. I really did not know what I was getting into but I went with him. We arrived at an apartment house of sorts and there were quite a few people there, some of which were from our town. They were there for one thing: heroin. I was the only one there who was so young, but Jim convinced them that they need not fear my presence; that I was 'cool'. I was not interested in their drugs at all, but I watched them running heroin and watched their behavior after a hit. They were mellow. Finally Jim convinced me to let him hit me with a small dose of heroin. He did not ever want me to do it the second time; he just wanted me to feel what it was like just once. I let him do it to me; what a fool I was. I did not belong in this place. The drug is notorious to make you vomit and that I did. The feeling was mellow but the price one pays is too great and the feeling is just that: a feeling. Feelings go away. I never touched the stuff again and never wanted to.

By this time I had given up on trying to keep up my attendance at school. I was either very late for my first class or I just never showed up. My first class teacher let me walk into her class late and never said a word. I kept trying, but I think I did not have an alarm clock and just never woke up in time. I really don't know what I was eating. I was cooking over a camp fire. I probably did not smell very good, either. Jim was pursuing me on a daily basis and finally I just never went back to school.

I could not continue to live in this hut in the woods. I was on somebody's property and I had to do something else. I really had no options so I went back to my parent's house. They always let me come home without a big fuss.

I needed a job and there was an opening at a physical therapy department at the hospital. I knew the therapist; she was the mother of an old friend. So I applied and got the job. It was a good job. I was very strong in my arms and hands, so I gave good massages. I like people; especially the old folks. I enjoyed helping them. I stayed with the job for a long period. It paid pretty good and I saved money. So I decided to rent a house as far out in the country as I could find. I drove out in the rural areas and asked old farmers if they knew of any vacant houses. I could fix up about anything. Well, I found a house that had long since been abandoned, but it had windows and doors that shut, and a chimney. It was gettin' on toward winter so the chimney was an important feature. There was no running water, but there was a well in the back yard that I hoped to get a hand pump on. I got to know the neighbors, who were quite a distance away; they were all nice to me. They gave me bags of sweet potatoes and turnips. I visited them, sat around their wood stove, drank hot tea and talked about all kinds of things. I liked them and they liked me. They were a family that lived in a few houses close to each other and made for a small community.

I bought me a big ol' pot-belly stove and got it all hooked up. There was electricity there and I used a hot plate to cook on along with the wood stove. I kept a pot of sassafras tea going constantly on the stove. I bought a rick of wood and with a lot of furniture from home, I set up house. I am an artist and had a collection of paintings which I put up in the various rooms. The house was fairly large. It had rough-cut boards as the walls and I liked the way it looked, but it was cold: there was no insulation in the walls. Nevertheless, I loved it there. I cooked big pots of beans and in a cast iron Dutch oven I made corn bread on the pot-belly stove. I put lots of honey and butter on my corn bread. I was in hog heaven.

I drove a '51 flat bed Chevy truck with big ol' tires. It was a four speed-in-the-floor with a granny gear. My road, on which I was the only person that lived, was quite washed out. I didn't think anybody else could get down there but me unless they had granny gear.

I wasn't all alone, as I brought my dog and my sister's dog to live with me. My dog's name was Mad Dog, and my sister's was Duke. My dog was a German shepherd cross: a pretty big dog. Duke was a hybrid wolf. He was gray like a timber wolf and he acted like one. When we all went for a stroll, instead of following along or taking the lead like any dog would, he stayed just out of sight in the woods and stalked us.

I went to the auction, picked up a few laying hens and fixed them up a laying house in the "back yard", which really wasn't a yard, but more like the woods. I was situated up on a mountain. A large river valley sorta circled around a few miles away. I use to take my bamboo flute, sit on the back porch and play to the woods and the mountain. Duke would howl when I played; he howled just like a wolf.

The house was cold at night but I had an electric blanket and lots of covers. The dogs slept with me on the bed. One night it began to snow. I stoked up the stove, climbed under my covers, and fell fast asleep. All of a sudden I sat bolt straight up in bed and my feet were on the floor in a split second; there was a glow coming from the kitchen. Duke was already pacing the floor. Mad Dog was still on my bed. I ran in my thin nightgown and bare feet to the kitchen. The wall and ceiling near the chimney was on fire! I ran for the front door and to the yard to grab the rain barrel, which was just a wash tub under the water spout from the roof. As soon as the front door was opened Duke flew out and disappeared into the woods. Mad Dog was beside me. I ran with the tub to the kitchen and threw the water up on the fire, but to no avail. I knew I had little time to get out what was most important. The wall that was on fire held a painting which I jerked off the wall, ran for the front porch and tossed it into the yard. I ran through the house and got all the paintings and tossed them into the yard. I was running in and out fast. I grabbed the stereo which had a record on the turntable. I set the stereo on the porch and ran for more. I went into the extra room which had the staircase to the attic, where obviously the fire started. For lack of a closet I had hung a rail across the staircase and all my clothes were hanging there. I had a lot of old wool coats that were my mother's when she was young. I spread my arms wide and enclosed the whole lot of the clothes, lifting them all at once to get the hangers off the rail. I was able to get them all, but the flames were so close that the collars of the coats were already partly burned. I took them all and threw them on the front yard. Then I ran to the bedroom and started jerking out drawers from the dressers and throwing whole drawers on the front yard. All this time Mad Dog never left my side. The smoke was so bad in the top half of the house, and so thick I could not run in and out standing up because I could not breathe. I shut the door to the extra room that had the staircase to the attic because it was in flames. I had to think clearly at this point. It was only the mercy of God that I had any presence of mind. I knew I had to get out and get out fast. Bein' my last trip in was to the kitchen. I had to get the key to the truck, my big wool coat, my purse and $200.00 in a vase on the kitchen table. I grabbed these things and was struggling to make it to the front door to get out. Mad Dog was right beside me. As I passed the door to the extra room that I had shut, I heard my cat yowling in there. I could not save her; I could not breathe nor dare open the door. I made it out of the house and to my truck. I could not stop to pull anything away from the house or even off the front porch. I started up my truck and raced up that road faster than I thought possible and yelled for the neighbors to come and try to save my house. The men dressed quickly and several households were alerted. There was even a fire truck for that community and all these men drove down there. I was told to stay with the women. I was barefooted. My feet and hands were burned; my nylon night gown was melted in spots. I was traumatized so the women comforted me. I finally drove back down there but only to see the last of the house burn to the ground. There was nothing they could do to save it, but they bravely retrieved the items on the front porch. The stereo was in working order but the record on the turn table was melted. The men saved everything that I threw out on the yard. I was very thankful. Mad Dog was nearby but Duke was long gone. I was welcomed at the neighbors'. A daughter who lived alone had an extra bedroom and offered me a place until I decided what I was going to do. I had to call into work the next day that my house had burned down and I could not make it in. I took a few days to recover. The lady who took me in was kind. She was a Christian. She talked to me about God and read to me from the Bible.

I had to go back right away to look for Duke. I had put out some dog food and water in an old dilapidated barn that was on the place. There were signs he had been back there. I spent a lot of time calling him; I had Mad Dog with me, hoping that he would find Duke. I rummaged through the rubble to see what I could find. I salvaged my cast iron Dutch oven, but it was not useable anymore. Some pottery that my little sister and I had made in high school was still intact; only the glaze had changed colors. It was time to leave and still no Duke. So we left, knowing we had to come back the next day. We did that and finally Duke came to my calling. I was so happy to see him and he was so happy to see us.

I stayed on with the neighbors for a few weeks. Word got around town that my house had burned down. Then word got to these good neighbors of mine that I was seeing a married man. This was devastating news to these people because they were Christians. The daughter who had taken me in was faced with a hard decision. Because of her faith in God she could not continue to keep me in her home. She was crying when she told me. I only understood in part. I did not understand that my relationship with Jim was wrong. All I knew was that I loved him and he loved me, with that I thought it was right for us to be together. God was trying to teach me, but my love for Jim blinded my eyes. Nevertheless I had love and respect for this woman who had been so kind to me, and we parted as friends. I had no other options but to return to my parents' house. That was hard because things were not good between me and my parents. But they did not scold me even though I lost some of their old antique furniture. I had lost a lot of my belongings with theirs, too.

3.
BUSTED

As time went on I was still seeing Jim. He and another war vet named Harry became friends and drug partners. Harry had a girlfriend named Sally and they all were into hittin' drugs. But soon we all came down with Hepatitis. Back in those days they did not recognize the Hepatitis C virus. It came back from 'Nam with the soldiers and these vets had it. And they were not careful with their needles and shared them at least with their friends. Jim had shared his needle with me when he hit me with the heroin. We all were experiencing the acute stage of Hepatitis C. Sally was hospitalized and some others too. But I was not, nevertheless I was sick and with 'Hep' you are really sick. You have to be on complete bed rest for a month or more. But we all recovered from this acute stage of Hepatitis C and went on our way, not knowing that we would carry this virus with us for a life time. To this day I do not know if the others are still alive, but I did hear that some of their buddies were dead from Hepatitis C.

These men became desperate and began to rob drug stores. I pled with Jim to stop this stupidity, but he would not. One night they were determined to find morphine and set out with a plan that was dangerous and foolish. I was determined to stop them from this foolishness, so I got into the car along with Sally and Harry. We did talk them out of the plan to deter the only sheriff in a small town, but they proceeded to break into a doctor's office. They were not successful and went on to another town. All this we two girls had not bargained for. But we could not get out of it by this point; these two men were determined.

Their attempt in the next town was successful and came out with all kinds of drugs, but not what they really wanted; morphine. When we arrived at the little house we were renting they ran the drugs in their veins. These kinds of drugs were not made to be injected. My boyfriend Jim would sometimes fall on the floor, unconscious, and I would give him CPR. When I knew he was breathing I would keep my fingers on his pulse until the dawn. Then I felt I could rest easy. I was kind of the nurse maid for them all because I did not partake in these drugs; it was so totally against my morals. I tried to keep them eating good food. I remember waking them all up to breakfast of oatmeal. They were hard to wake up in the mornings.

This house we were renting in the country was very run down. We tried to clean it up and make it livable. We did that. It had beautiful wood trim inside, but it was scary to me. I remember thinking there were ghosts. I hung a bag of garlic over the door, to ward off evil spirits. Little did I know that, that was nonsense and our sinful life only invited evil spirits into our house. I often found myself alone in the house and that was frightening to me. There was nothing good about what we were doing there. I was only seventeen at this time. In spite of my ignorance I had a certain sense that the stealing and the drugs were very wrong and I did want no part of it. It all was so against my morals.

Not many days passed and the other three were constantly hitting these drugs. I'm sure the police were looking for the thieves. One day Harry and Sally were driving on the highway and they had a bunch of the drugs in their possession. They were stoned and I don't know if they were driving badly, but the police were onto them and turned on the sirens. I think they threw the drugs out the window, but they were pulled over and arrested; the police found the drugs and they were put in jail in the court house in town.

Sally was from a well-to-do family and her parents got her out quickly. The police bargained with her that if she would divulge the others involved in the burglary that she would get off with just probation. She did this so it was not long after that Jim was also arrested, but he was jailed in the town where the burglary took place. The jail was in the second floor of the courthouse, which was the center of the 'square' as we called it. Lawn surrounded the courthouse and then all the towns' stores made a square around the courthouse. I heard that Jim was in jail so I hitched there to see if I could talk to him. I stood down on the lawn and hollered up to him. He came to the window and we talked quite well that way. But pretty soon the sheriff came out and arrested me, too. I was placed in the women's cell on the same second floor. The walls of the court house formed a 45 degree angle and our windows were caddy corner to each other so we could talk back and forth. I was quite pleased with this arrangement. I had a pleasant attitude and was quite friendly with all of the guards. I suppose this was strange to them. I was just glad to be company for Jim as he was in real big trouble. Meals were pretty good. They brought hamburgers from a café somewhere. I stayed in there only a few days until my folks found out where I was. They came to bail me out, but I did not want to go. I still hated my parents. They were planning a trip to visit relatives the next day and had to get special permission to take me out of state. This was granted and I had no choice but to go with them.

Busted

Jim and Harry were convicted of burglary and grand larceny, and sentenced to two years in the state penitentiary. It was hard farm labor for them with all the horrors of prison life.

Sally and I were put on probation for one year as we were only charged with being accessories to the burglary. We both were faithful to report to our probation officers. We got jobs and were rewarded for our good behavior.

When I turned eighteen, I was released from probation and my record was cleared. My dad and I attended the court in a town quite far away from home. That was a long time ago and I do not know what all was in my mind, but I decided to leave home and seek work. So my dad dropped me off on the side of the highway with my bed roll and a little food in my pack. He said he envied me because I was so free. I knew some people in a town a few hours away and decided I would hitchhike there. Amongst these friends was a lady named Crystal that I got to know. She and I decided to go back to my home town to look for work. So we set out hitching. We got picked up by some hillbillies that were going to leave the next day for the west to pick apples. They told us anyone could get work, so we asked if we could ride along. They said yes in spite of the fact they were three young men and us two young ladies and their car was a Mustang. We drove straight through. It was miserable. I remember trying to stretch out in the back window. Nevertheless they were respectful and we arrived safely. We were dropped off in a bigger town that I would call a city. After visiting a job service outfit and a food bank we decided to hitch north and follow the apples. We did this and met other pickers waiting for the season to kick off. In the mean time we camped in a high mountain primitive camp area. There was a reservoir there of clean and shockingly cold water. We were there a week or two and then the apples started up. We got a job and an old house for shelter while we picked.

When I left my dad that day on the highway, I had stressed I did not want anyone to know where I was. I guess I did not want Jim to find me when he got out of prison. If only I had been strong in my decision my whole life would have turned out so much better. One bad decision in a weak moment a person can pay for, for the rest of their life.

My little sister Ellie was the only one who knew where I was. I remember calling her from a pay phone in a camp ground. She told me Jim wanted to contact me. He had gone back to his wife when he was released from prison, but it was me that he loved and he wanted to come to me. This meant jumping parole. I allowed her to give him the phone number of the camp ground and had him call at a certain time and I would be there. Talking to him was a weakening and since I loved him I gave into this proposal. He did come to where I was. Oh what a mistake.

4.

ABANDONED

I became pregnant. We picked apples that season and then when it was all over, we rented a house until our money ran out. We tried to get work but there just wasn't anything we could do. We had purchased an old car, really old. We were not use to winters in the north and really had no idea how to survive. For a little while a nice family took us in, but we soon decided to leave to go to Alabama where we knew a couple of apple pickers and were college students. They offered us a place to live 'till we could get settled. Alabama was a long way away. But we set out across the Dakotas in winter. The window in the car did not have good seals and the wind was blowing snow sideways and right into the car. It was night and zero degrees, and we were nearly out of gas. Finally we came to a town. Everything was closed, but we could go no further. We had a dog with us that someone had given me on a hitching hiking tour on the west coast. So we all settled into the back seat to sleep until morning. We all lived through the night. But the dog's eye lids were frozen shut. Thank goodness the baby was not yet born and stayed warm in my womb.

Deliverance from Oppression

We made it to Illinois and the car broke down. We had no money to fix it. The mechanic knew a Christian family who would take us in. We pretended to be married. While in their home Jim was making private phone calls. He lied about to whom and I suppose I believed him. After two weeks this Christian family offered us an old station wagon that did run. We took it gladly and made it to Alabama. As we arrived at the apple pickers' apartment, the engine blew up. So we were stranded again. That night the phone rang and it was for Jim. This was strange and I still was naive. Soon he said he was walking down to the corner grocery store for cigarettes and I was to stay at the apartment. He never came back. He had this planned all along. His wife was living in Florida with their two children and she had a job. He loved his children and she provided a secure home always and so continued my same old story of rejection and abandonment. But this time it was multiplied in devastating degrees. I was pregnant. I had no home, no job and no money.

I spent my days looking out the window while my friends were at college. I cried and cried and was having pains in my belly. I thought I was going to lose the baby. The feeling of abandonment and hopelessness is so dark. There was no light and I am sure I talked with God but I did not know Him. I was swallowed up in sin and the wages of such a life is death. I don't know how much time went by before I stepped out of my gloom, but it seemed forever. Nor did I imagine that what I felt, my little son in my womb also felt. These feelings were being imprinted in his mind as well as my own and would affect our future.

Soon I met some people who were selling flowers on the street corner. I was able to get a job doing this as well. They lived in an apartment some blocks away and said I could park my car in an alley across the street and use the bathroom in their house. So we towed the car to the alley and I took up residence. The car was a station wagon so I made a bed in the back and put up curtains as best as I could. The glove compartment door was my kitchen table. With a little money I could buy some groceries and dog food at the corner grocery. I also learned of a women's' clinic that provided prenatal vitamins for free, so I was able to take vitamins during my pregnancy. I was about four or five months along at that time. I was very glad for my dog since she was a purebred German Shepherd. My location was in the poor section of town. I think people have a certain respect for a German Shepherd, so anyone who might have been watching this ordeal gave me space to carry on.

5.

MY FIRST SON

Time went on and I was so sad, and so desperate. But I was alive and trying to eat as well as I could with no refrigeration. Somehow Jim got a hold of me. Of course he was so sorry for leaving me and wanted to be with me again. So he finally returned to me and together we sold flowers on the street corner, and lived in the station wagon. But I did not supply a secure home for him and I could not get the drugs that he required for his epilepsy. And then of course there were his two little girls who just did not understand why their daddy was always gone. Later he told me that he knew he could not provide for me and I was about to have a baby. So once again he snuck away and abandoned me in that big city, living in the back of a station wagon parked in an alley in the poor section of town. I was devastated and sad.

Soon I knew that I had no choice but to call my parents, I told them I was going to have a baby, and I had no home. My dad said he would come get me and he was there the next day. He drove straight through both ways. I was amazed that my dad never lectured me or insulted me. He told me I could live at home and they would pay for the delivery. They had a new home that they built in the country and

My first Son

the setting was very pleasant. My relationship with them changed from that time forward.

I bore my first son two days after my nineteenth birthday. The delivery was difficult. My little sister Ellie and my mom were close by. But my baby was strong, I was strong and we did well. I named him after his father, but he carried my last name. I nursed him and I loved him very much. My parents supported me as long as was needful. But then a phone call came when the baby was about two months old. It was Jim. He explained that he had to do what he did for the baby's sake but that now he wanted to be with us. He was still wanted by the law in our home state. Well my little sister Ellie was wantin' to move to Arizona so we decided to go there and start a new life. We met Jim at a Greyhound station in the next state and then we went to Arizona. I was nursing so I could not get a job. Ellie worked, but Jim never did. He never could hold a job or tried very hard to get one. Soon I found a babysitting job where I could take my son with me. That did not last long.

Jim told me he had divorced his wife prior to this adventure, and I believed him. But he lied. In the end I was so thankful that we never married. My life was so devastated by this relationship it was good it was not furthered by a real legal marriage.

One night on Jim's birthday he wanted to go to the tavern to celebrate. Of course I could not go because I had the baby. But I rode along and sat in the car. It was night and we parked on the square along the courthouse lawn. He and my sister went in and I waited. It was a cold winter night. As they returned they walked across the courthouse lawn. All of a sudden and out of nowhere there were policemen yelling "Freeze"! They had spot lights on them and guns pointed at them. Of course they froze. Jim was arrested and my sister was free to go. They took him to jail. He was extradited back to our home state and sent back to prison. My little sister Elle and I returned to our home town and settled in and got jobs.

6.

I HAD A PLAN

I was faithful to Jim all that next year that he was imprisoned. I wrote letters everyday and visited him at the state penitentiary almost every visiting day, which was twice a month. I stood in those long lines to get inside to a visitation auditorium, for an hour with my baby boy in my arms. The drive was four hours one way. I had to leave home early in the morning and it was often foggy and raining. I was driving an older, sorta worn-out car of my folks. Back in those days windshield wipers operated on a vacuum motor. Well the vacuum had about had it; it took the wipers one direction but not the other. So I tied bailing twine to the wiper arm and fed the rope through my wing window so I could pull the rope. So the motor pulled the wipers to the down position and I pulled them to the up position. This was very precarious, as I was trying to traverse the highway which was up and down and this way and that way, all the while cooing to my little baby boy in the back seat. I always kept the radio going and listened to a Christian radio station and this is where I really began to realize that I needed God in my life. But my understanding was so feeble and I loved Jim. I was blinded to the sin I was living in. I don't think I could grasp that this was adultery and separated me from God. But there was a live ember in my heart for God and He loved me more than I understood. I am so grateful He kept me alive and waited for me.

When Jim was released from prison over a year later, I had rented a house and awaited him to come to me. By this time our son was one and my mother cared for him while I worked at the factory. I worked second shift so I could be home with little Jimmy most all day. But as it turned out, to be released from prison a man has to have work lined up and a home ready waiting for him. And his wife had all this done, unbeknownced to me. She and I worked at the same factory in the same department. When he came home and never came to me, I was devastated. I actually drove to her house one night and stood outside and cried 'till I collapsed. I never went to the door. I'm not sure what my intention was.

Finally I let the house go that I had rented and moved back in with my parents. Time passed and the child grew, was happy and very lively. My mother and he bonded well. She loved him as her own. I continued to work and save money.

Soon Jim contacted me and we began to see each other again. We rented cabins occasionally so we could be a family. But he drank and used up all the money I could earn and we were always kicked out.

His addictions became more devastating and he became a desperate and violent man. I, being a person who stood for the right became his victim. He beat me many times and mostly in the presence of our little son. This was terror for me and terror for the child. Jimmy and I escaped for our lives time and again, packing all our stuff and fleeing. But he found us and begged us to come back to him, pleading that I was his only link to God and he loved me. I forgave him and believed what he said. He always promised he would stop drinking and he never did, ever. We were often homeless, hungry and destitute. Though I held a job, he could not seem to keep any job. The money I made he demanded I give it to him. If I would not, he stole it out of my purse and bought more beer. We could never keep up rental payments on a house. Even an old truck with a camper shell in which we lived was sold for $50.00 to buy more beer.

He robbed another doctor's office and got caught in the act. But his wife got him out on bond. Knowing he would be imprisoned again he decided to skip the state. So we rode along with some folks who wanted to pick apples and headed north. I knew apple pickers where we were going and I was taking advantage of the opportunity to get back to some people who could help me get away from this man.

We took nicknames because Jim was wanted by the law. We picked apples that season and bought a teepee as something we would always have to provide our own shelter. It was brand new; the only thing we owned of value as everything else had been sold for more beer. This way of life was so far from my morals and convictions that finally after becoming a mother, I wanted stability. I was a hard worker; I could make money, save it and spend it wisely. My parents taught me all that and I am thankful for that foundation. What was taking place in my life was not acceptable to me and I had a plan of escape....again.

While picking apples that season we met a man who owned land up on a mountain in the country. He offered to us the opportunity to set up our teepee and winter on his land. Being from the south we did not clue in to what life was like in this north country, in the winter up on a mountain, much less in a teepee! But we had no other option so we went for it. Snow had not yet come, so we cut poles for the teepee and set it up with much trial. Jim was never able to take on a task and master it. He would always yell and cuss and blame me, then quit. I hated being around someone so unstable, incapable and dangerous. Finally the teepee stood and we attempted to install a wood heat stove in the center, semi-buried to give heat to the floor level. This task turned out to be disastrous. Our little son was blessed by the land owner to be able to stay in his cabin by the stove while we did all this. Thank God in Heaven for providing and protecting little children, fore out in the teepee all hell broke loose. Jim began to beat me and kick in my ribs. To say the least we never got the teepee livable. I remember just sleeping on the floor of this landowner's cabin, ah....by the stove. Next day this mountain man and Jim decided to go to town for beer. I opted to stay at the cabin with my little boy. I had a plan.

7.
STUFFING THE GUNNYSACKS

As soon as they were gone I ran to the teepee and stuffed gunnysacks full of our clothes and dragged them to the side of the dirt road. Bein's that it was hunting season I had hopes someone would come by. Sure enough two hunters came by and I put up my thumb. They stopped, kindly obliged me to take Jimmy and me to the valley, and dropped us on the main highway. We hitched to a town about three hours south where I used to pick apples and knew some pickers. I found them and they took us in. They were devastated that I had been undergoing these beatings and they were determined to hide me. But unfortunately Jim knew the location of these pickers and he soon found us there. I refused to go back to him so he was going to head back to the mountain where the teepee was. I had to go back north to an appointment. Next morning Jimmy and I went to the side of the highway heading for our appointment, and who showed up to hitch with us but Jim. He begged me to let him hitch with us as he could never get rides alone. I couldn't get rid of him, so when the first car stopped, he jumped in with us. And from there he never would leave our sight. I was stuck again.

After the appointment we all went back to the teepee to gather clothing and food and hitch to the valley where we could look for work and a house because living on a mountain in a teepee just was not working. We had a bicycle that we wanted to sell for a little money, but it bought mostly beer. We were standing on the street of this small town at dark in November with our little boy, hungry and cold and nowhere to go. Of course Jim was always angry and yelling. That never helped things. I wish that I was sensitive enough to my little son at that time to really grasp what this existence was doing to his mind and heart. He must have been terrified; he was only three. I guess, though, in the long vision I was determined to escape and provide a stable life for him and me. I was getting there. But this journey was gruesome.

That night I got on a phone and called a local church. We hitched to the preacher's house and he set us up for some nights in a picker's shack. Ah... a bed and wood stove; we were saved once again. The orchard owner offered Jim a job in a little packing shed of which he was part owner of. So next day he went to work. I was planning my escape. This was perfect, I could leave him here; he would have a job, a cabin and I could get away.

We needed more of our things from the teepee. When Jim returned from work he decided to ask a fellow worker to take him to the teepee on the week end. So I waited. We actually had a puppy that we had left with the mountain man and we really needed to go up there. I stayed back with Jimmy and they went up there. Well the person who offered to go was an older lady and a drinker. So they both were drinking and on the way back down the mountain, almost to the valley town where we were living; there was an accident. She drove a small light weight car and was driving fast. They went over an embankment on the edge of town and rolled it to the bottom. Jim was thrown from the car and lived with minor injuries. The woman did not live. When he was dismissed from the hospital he told me the sad story. How horrible!

To say the least our things were strewn over that canyon side, including the puppy. So I went to the area searching for our things. I gathered up our stuff, and then went door to door in the neighborhood asking if anyone had found a puppy. No one had. But I met some people who when I told my story I trusted to really tell them the whole story. They said that they would help me. They knew of a vacant cabin in the mountains that I could winter in. So I told them I would return as soon as Jim went back to work. And that I did. The first day that he was able to work I stuffed our gunnysacks with all our belongings and dragged them to the side of the road and put up my thumb. An older gentleman stopped and was obliged to take us to the door of the people who said they would help us. God was watching over us even though I did not "know" Him.

These folks took us straight to this mountain cabin. It was winter and cold, and when I got out of the car to walk up to the door, I considered that I did not have money or tools to cut and chop wood. I knew we would never make it. I knew that the apple picker, who was my friend, had moved to a town about sixty miles away so I asked these folks if they would take me there. They agreed and dropped us off at the general store of that little town. I inquired there of the ranch where my friend had moved. They directed me, so with my son and our gunnysacks, I stuck out my thumb once again and we made it to the farm. And indeed I found my friend living in a teepee with about two feet of snow surrounding it. He welcomed us warmly. His fire was indeed warm and the teepee was well set up with a wooden floor slightly elevated above the stove. We stayed there securely for a while.

8.

SERENITY SHATTERED

*B*eing from the south this cold climate was more than I had ever imagined. And the snow never melted 'till spring. Living in a teepee one could never escape the cold and the reality of snow. There was a cabin on the farm that was needin' a roof; otherwise was finished. It was round and small but already had a big pot-bellied stove inside. It had three picture windows looking out over the mountainside. I asked permission to finish it and live there for the time bein'. The owners of the farm agreed. One man offered to help me. In time Jimmy and I were moved in and warm we were. Our own little cabin! It had a big table in the center where I prepared food. We cooked on the pot- bellied stove. The floor was bedded with pine needles for a carpet. It was soft for sleeping on. I even had a rocking chair in there. We were secure, or so it felt for a while.

There were several cabins, or lodges as they called them, built all over the farm land. I suppose some people would call this a hippie commune. I met all the families. One lady and I became fast friends and our boys played together. Our cabins were just a holler away.

Life was pleasant on the farm and winter was beautiful looking out the window of my cabin. But after a month my serenity was shattered. He found me, and came there demanding I forfeit the brand new teepee we had purchased with our apple picking money. I refused because it was a secure home for me and Jimmy in the future. Everything we ever owned of value he sold for more beer or drugs. I was standing my ground when he shoved me down and broke my leg. The folks on the farmstead witnessed this event from the window of their house that snowy night in November. I had to crawl to the safety of their house. They came outside, gave Jim the teepee and told him to leave; he did. These folks took me to the emergency room and a cast was put on my leg. They took care of me and Jimmy until I could return to my cabin.

One night I came home on the donkey which was lead by a neighbor, bein's I could not hike in the deep snow due to my broken leg. We had gone up the mountain to another home where we had supper and fellowship. When we returned to my cabin, my neighbor left me assured I was okay. I went to the outhouse on my crutches and returned to the cabin. I entered and lit the lantern and there was Jim waiting in the dark of my cabin that snowy winter night. He had come to kill me. He said if he could not have me, no one would have me.

I sat helpless in the presence of this man who many times said he loved me but now was here to kill me. There was no chance of running for my life because of my broken leg and the snow was three feet deep. I asked him if he brought a gun, and he said, "No, I don't need one". I kept making excuses to go to the outhouse just in case I would hear someone walking down the trail. But it was in the middle of the night and all was quiet. I negotiated with him all through the night and he agreed that if I gave him money, he would leave the state to work the fruit in Florida. At dawn I hobbled down the steep trail to the neighbors' to ask for money and they were obliged to help. My little son Jimmy was spared the trauma of that night because he was staying the night with his little friends at the main farm house.

A decision had to be made and everyone gathered who lived on the farm. They decided it would be too risky to give him money. He could always return and try this again. For my safety they decided to call the police. Jim was wanted from our home state because he had jumped bond. The state opted to extradite him, so the local sheriff came and got him. He went willingly for fear of being shot in the back. We were finally safe from him. He went back to prison.

We thought we were free from him, but many years later I received a phone call in the middle of the night; it was New Year's Eve. As I answered the call and heard his voice I was in terror. He spoke so softly. He said he wanted to wish me happy New Year's and talk about old times. I told him old times were a nightmare to me and to never, ever call me again, and I hung up. I immediately was in fight-and-flight: Post Traumatic Stress. I was terrified that he found me again. I imagined he would come to my house. I planned that if he came to the front door, I would escape out the back door and flee through the fields to the neighbors'. If he came to the back door, I would flee out the front and cross the low land to the other neighbors'. I planned to change my phone number the next morning. I went to bed with my boots next to the bed along with warm clothes in case I had to run in the night. When I knelt down next to my bed to say my prayers, I leaned my heart against the bed. It felt like my heart was collapsing. I was losing my breath and my extremities were tingling. I realized that my brain was reacting as if this drama was happening right then. I reasoned with myself that I was reliving the past and this was not happening right then. My brain was activated in the present and sending signals as if I should be ready to run. I gathered myself and began to use my logical brain; I started talking out loud to my heart. I said, "Heart, be calm.

This is not happening now, I do not need to run and I do not need to be afraid. Be calm. All this is in the past. Jesus is here and all is well". Right away I felt my pulse beginning to slow down. I laid flat on the bed and spread my arms out to take the pressure off my heart and increase the circulation to my limbs. Soon the tingling subsided and I continued to talk peace to my heart out loud. This worked very well. Soon I was calm and my body was back to normal. Later I fell asleep. This method to overcome these flash backs and panic worked wonderfully in the years that followed. I had suffered from nightmares for many years, dreaming of escape. Jims' face would appear in a dream that was pleasant and my guard was down. He had found me again and I was trapped. But I think that this entry of new data self talk into my brain helped to override fear and decrease even the nightmares.

The next morning I was determined to change my phone number and I heard the Lord speak to me. He said, "Be not afraid. I will take care of you". I knew there was nothing to be afraid of after that and I let go of the fear. I never received any more phone calls from him after that and we were never bothered by him again.

The damage that relationship did to my person and my mind, I never knew at that time. The damage that was done to my son in the formative years of his brain development was unknown to me as well. I think in those days they did not understand Post Traumatic Stress Disorder. There were not "women's shelters" that I had heard of. Nor through it all did I ever seek another person to talk to, until I trusted those folks I met after the wreck when I was looking for my puppy. I can't analyze where I was in my mind during those years, but today I still suffer the damage to my mind, body and spirit. Over forty years have passed.

9.

OVER THE MOUNTAIN

    Being a farmer at heart I purchased a horse which was un-broke, and a donkey of which I have already spoken of. I also traded for three goats and some sheep skins that would be our beds. In the trade was included a two-man cross-cut saw and a bow saw. I was ready to set up my farmstead. When spring came some of us opted to move to a new community about thirty miles to the west. The thought for this community was a place for healing. A "Healing Gathering" was in the making for that spring. This community was in its developmental stage but the land was purchased and the door was open for members to move in. I attended a few meetings and was welcomed. So in early April I set out walking with my horse and pack donkey. I was going to leave the goats and my son with friends at the farm until I could get set up. I was to leave in the morning alone. But my friend's husband decided I could not go it alone so he offered to assist me. He led the un-broke horse and carried a back pack. I led the donkey, which was fully packed with food and bedding. I had only recently gotten the cast off my leg and was still walking with a walking stick. We had a map and decided to take a mountain pass Forest

Service road that cut miles off the journey. Only problem was, we did not consider the time of year and the elevation. I was from the south and had a lot to learn.

We made it to the bottom of the east slope of the mountain the first day and a farmer took us in for the night. He was a wood carver and gave us each a spoon made of wood; I kept that spoon for years and used it as my only eating utensil.

Leaving the next morning, we began to climb in elevation and were coming into the snow line. Soon it was snowing a blizzard. I could no longer walk with my cane so I stuck it in my pack saddle and trudged on through the deep snow. It was so deep that it came up to the donkeys' belly. He had to rear and leap with each stride, fully packed. Oh, he worked so hard. We thought we would never make it to the top, and begin our descent into the valley in which lay the community we were striving for. I don't remember it bein' very cold and it was lovely. The snow was falling softly and the flakes were large. We actually saw some tracks of some other hikers that were going the same way as we were. We later found out who they were. They left the trail and went cross-country and came right down on to "the land", as we called it.

There were little snow birds twittering through the trees, it was so beautiful and peaceful up on that mountain. But we were laboring profusely. My friend was carrying a seventy pound back pack. This was getting serious. Finally we stopped going up. It was near evening so we made camp. We built a fire and cooked a good hearty supper. It was still snowing so we took the canvas that covered our pack on the donkey and laid it on the snow and put our sleeping bags inside and then folded the tarp over our bags and heads and let it snow. We stayed warm and dry and the animals rested. We fed them and we were ready to start out fresh the next morning.

Our descent was a breeze and we were soon out of the snow. What a relief! The first farm we came to was neighboring to our land. We stopped and they gave us directions and told us others had shown up a few days before. There was an old dilapidated two-story house there and I was able to tie the animals and bed down inside. My friend showed up in their truck to pick up her husband. They left me and went home but they kept my son for two weeks along with the goats.

So my first night was alone in this dilapidated old house, but I settled in and tried to sleep when I heard, "Thump, thump, thump". Something rather large, I would say, was coming down the old stair case. Well it turned out that there were quite a few other residents in that old house such as marmots, pack rats and the like. It was rather scary. I laid there for a while and then I heard voices; people! Yes, they came down from a camp up higher and were walking the two miles into the little town to the tavern to have some munchies and beer. They came to invite me! And was I ever ready to go. I made sure the horses were secure and we walked into town. The tavern was warm and friendly, and hardly anyone there. I think when I returned I could sleep better.

These people were very idealistic and did not like barbwire fences so horses were not really part of their dream. My plan was to go just above the property on forest land and set up a camp and graze my horses. The next day I set out to find a camp, one with water of course. I made a camp, but not with water. I set up a small teepee with the canvas I had and made a fire pit in the middle. I covered it with a grate and then hung my duffle bag of food from the teepee poles. Nice camp, but the horses did not think so. They left and headed down hill to water and ended up at the neighboring farm. I went looking for them and found them. So my little camp never went over. I eventually rented a pasture for them not too far from the land. Just until the horse people found their allotted niche. When I returned for my stuff at my camp, well, I'm glad I wasn't there when this visitor came to make himself at home. He stepped on the grate in the center of the teepee and pulled down the duffel bag of food, drug it some distance and opened it up and strewed the food across the mountainside. The honey jar was gone. He must have been rather large because the grate was bent in half like a V. So I moved in with some mothers who had arrived on the land and set up a large teepee down on the bottom land in the aspen trees. There was a creek and a spring that we could get our water nearby. It was good to be able to get out of the rain and warm up and cook our food over a fire.

I was in the market for one more horse and set out on a quest to see if I could find one. My dear friend from the ranch we lived on prior to coming to the land, she and her family also needed one more riding horse. So her husband came with me. We were hitch-hiking. We put on some miles up and down a valley near the land, inquired with farmers and kept our eyes peeled. We spied a nice white Appy from the road and stopped to inquire about him. He was for sale and my companion bought him. The farmer that sold him to us told us where he bought him; from a Native Indian family up near the mountain range to our west. So we excitedly hitched up there and was it ever beautiful there! A large river ran through the ranch and the high mountains loomed up above. We talked to the elderly farmer. He said he would go and round up his herd for us so we could take a look at his stock, but it was too late that day. He invited us to stay the night, knowing we were on foot. We asked to just sleep in the barn but he would have no part of that. In his home were his wife, an older daughter and an older son with all his children. It was a full house; nevertheless he offered us to sleep on the couch, which was a hid-a-bed. But there were two of us and we were not married. They did not even consider the fact. It was either we both slept on the bed or one of us on the floor. Neither one of us wanted to sleep on the floor, so we slept on the bed together, keeping a respectable distance between us.

Next morning his wife and oldest daughter were up early and cooking breakfast. We scurried around, folded up our bed and prepared for the day. They had a long table off the kitchen and it was all set for the family and us. When we were all seated the women brought out the food. There were eggs, pancakes and bacon. The plate of eggs which were fried, was piled high and set in the middle of the table. The pancake plate was likewise. We feasted while we visited with this family. What a pleasant morning we had. Soon we were ready to head out to find the horses. The grandfather sent his ten year old grandson and a younger granddaughter to saddle up two riding horses that were pastured near the house. As the children saddled and headed out to round up the herd, we followed in so far, in the pickup. The children kicked their horses into a full run and crashed through the river to the bottom land on the far side. We watched and waited for some time, and all the while we were tapping into the history of this old Indian man. We learned a lot about their ranch and their family. Eventually we saw the herd coming and it was being led by a pure white stallion. The grandfather told us he was a purebred Appaloosa but had turned white over the years. He was huge and if I remember correctly he told us he was seventeen hands high. The herd came crashing across the river and headed into the barn yard. The old grandfather caught the stallion and put him in the barn for our safety. He told us beside the brood mares, these younger horses had never been touched by human hands.

They herded the horses into a large paddock. I went in and moved amongst them. There were some Appaloosa mares and some mares that were a cross with Arab blood. I was able to pet this one sweet two-year-old filly. She was mostly white with black spots on her rump, and blackish below the knees. She looked almost identical to the one my companion bought in the valley. In fact they were half brother and sister. When I walked away from this filly and meandered amongst this herd, she followed me with her nose near touching my back. I turned to pet her again, I thought this is what she was asking for. I really wasn't thinking of purchasing her as she was quite small. She was only two years old and not ready to be ridden. This herd of horses was basically wild and was not fed regularly in the winter. I think this is why she was a bit small. So I continued looking the horses over and this filly continued to follow me. Soon I was convinced that she had bonded to me and perhaps I had bonded to her in just a few minutes. This horse had never been touched by human hands, I marveled. The decision was made, I wanted her.

So I discussed this with the old grandfather and he showed me which mare she came out of. The mare was not white but more a roan color. She was half Appy and half Arab. The stallion being full Appaloosa, this made the little filly three quarters Appaloosa and one quarter Arab. She had an Arab head, but her body was stocky, more after the Appy blood. I liked her a lot and soon I loved her. I asked the grandfather if I could make two payments for her, leaving her with him until she was paid in full. He was very glad to do this and I paid him half that day. He told me that he would leave her corralled and have his grandchildren get on her to make sure she did not buck. He later told me that he was able to get the saddle on her and she never bucked the children. So when I got her home my work was just training her about everything else that goes along with riding and domestic life in general. She trained easily and never in her life did she buck, rear, kick or bite. I called her the sweetest horse in the whole wide world. I owned her for twenty one years until she died of old age. She never had a foal, as I really did not need another horse. She served all my needs. I believe that if horses go to Heaven she will be there. I have never owned a horse that even compared to her and I don't think I ever will. I named her Fairy Dancer.

10.
BUILDING OUR LODGE

By this time my son and the goats were back with me on the land. I had chosen an old cattle shed with a roof line like an ol' sway back mare, for our homestead. I divided it off with the people on one side, and the hay and goats on the other side. It was the only wooden inhabited structure on the land. I put in a wood stove and we were warm. My coffee and pancakes attracted many a passersby and our little home became a center of attraction. The goats could stand on their hind legs and stick their noses over on our side. I enjoyed their company. The creek went right past us and the spring was about a stone throw away.

That spring I met a man named Lone Buck that I thought I could spend my life with. He was strong and wise and a hard worker. Though he was attracted to me he was not committed and soon left on a long journey.

As summer progressed the horse people dug a well and we, being three households, built lodges on a mountaintop where we were to live out of sight with our barbwire fences. My lodge was an earth lodge; I dug the hole with a shovel. The horse people grouped together with two-man cross cut-saws and went to the forest with an old '49 flat bed truck. We cut the timbers we needed for the structures and hauled them to our building sites. It was getting' on toward fall and there was a lot of work to be done. I stripped the logs and poles, and with my own design began the construction. Once in a while a volunteer would show up to give a hand to the horse people. It took about an hour to walk up there from below; most people were not that motivated. I was still living in the goat shed below on the creek, so I walked it every day to work.

The man whose name was Lone Buck, a nick name that his grandfather gave him because he was tall, strong and of noble character; returned before winter and helped to get the lodge finished. We decided it took too much energy to walk the mountain trail to the top where we were building the lodge. So we pitched a four-man canvas tent and put a pot-belly stove inside. We stayed warm in there as long as the stove was going, but when it went out, it was as cold inside as it was outside. But we had piles of blankets and sleeping bags. I piled them high on my little boy. He was a tough child and could walk up and down that mountain by himself. We were not financially set so we ate from a store house that was set up below for all to take part from. We had a fifty pound bag of oatmeal and had acquired some fat back from the neighbors hog farm. If you have never had fat back in oatmeal you should try it; it's good. This was kind of our mainstay. We had to build a little corral around the tent because the horses could come right up to where we were pitched. One day they tore the tent and had themselves some oatmeal. The tent had a few holes in the roof so we leaned a piece of plywood over that side of the peaked tent. The end was resting on the corral rail and then a wheel barrow leaned on the end of the plywood to hold the weight of it off the roof of the tent. It worked!

It was November and a lot of snow had already fallen. For two weeks while we lived in the tent it was minus twenty degrees at night. This was serious cold. We tried to keep the stove going and when we had it cranking it was so hot in there we had to strip down to our long johns. But on Thanksgiving Day we moved the tent in under the roof of the house. It was an underground house. The roof came right down to the dirt and only the south face was open; and the gable end to the north. We were protected from the wind and the earth gave some warmth. We directed the stove pipe out the gable end which really was the loft wall facing north; it had two small windows. We were thankful indeed to be in a protected and warmer spot. We all took baths in the wash tub and went down to the main lodge below for Thanksgiving dinner. When I refer to going below, I mean that there were most of the residents living below near the spring. They all were building winter shelter as we were up on the mountain. They called their shelter the long house. A lot of folks wintered there. They had a big heat stove and a cook stove. Lots of food was made for the meal that day. A root cellar was dug into the earth that was accessed from inside the long house. It was very well stocked with food. We feasted well into the night and then hiked up the mountain on our snowy trails. When Jimmy was sleepy he was either carried by Lone Buck, or put on the back of the pack donkey. Many a night we walked slowly up that mountain trail; sometimes there were no stars or moon to light the way. When everything is white it is hard to distinguish the trail. But the trail was ever so slightly darker in color so you could stay on it if you tried hard and paid attention. If you stepped off the packed part your boot would sink into soft snow up to your knees. We had a husky dog with a fluffy white tail. He often was out in the lead. We could follow the white tail and keep our boots on the packed part. But sometimes he was hard to keep up with.

    Every day we worked hard to close in the walls of the lodge. The days were only zero degrees. Jimmy would spend the days with his little friends where their lodge was completed while we worked on the house.

We wore lots of clothes and heavy gloves. Problem was it is hard to pick up a nail with heavy gloves. So we had to take off the glove, pick up a nail, set it with a hammer blow then put the glove back on to finish driving the nail. It was so cold that our fingers stuck to the metal of the nail. This made for slow progress. We used hand saws to cut the boards and any poles we were using. One day I was sawing a board with a cross-cut bow saw, holding the board with my left hand. The saw jumped out of the cut and cut my index finger. It was a jagged cut and a lot of blood. I fainted in the snow and Lone Buck carried me into the tent and bandaged me up. I was okay just needin' to get my head lower than my wound. I imagine I went back to work shortly.

During this time I developed pneumonia and was laid up for awhile. The tent was not the warmest hospital, but I had to rest. I drank hot herb teas and rubbed my chest with herbal concoctions. Soon I was able to get back to work.

Over the next weeks we made good progress and closed in the south wall. That included three picture windows. The front of the lodge to the south was three-sided; each held a picture window. Two were horizontal and the center one was perpendicular, which sent the window up toward the ridge pole, making light to the loft. The ground level was at about four feet on that side. The doorway came into the lodge from the east, facing an aspen grove just above the well. The doorway entrance was sorta like a tunnel without a roof. The floor and walls of the lodge were dirt. The A frame roof was settled on seal logs that sat outside the dirt walls. I fashioned an underground gutter system that carried away the water from the structure. The dirt walls always held firm. We completed the loft floor and hung tarps over the open side that faced into the lodge. We moved into the loft on Christmas Eve day. We went to the woods for a fir bough, hung it from a post and decorated it. We had presents for each other and it was a joyous Christmas. We were so thankful to be surrounded by wood, a wooden floor and a wall with two windows; one of which the stove pipe went out. The roof was wooden overhead. Jimmy was so happy that Christmas morning. We all were.

Finally the house was complete, other than insulation, which I worked on over the winter using three layers of corrugated cardboard. The doorway was just three heavy tarps weighted at the bottom. All the windows were installed, we had a big wood stove in the middle of the one room, and the loft extended over half the floor space. The overall dimensions were 24' x 15'. Now we were warm, and safe, and happy. It was New Year's Day. We all took baths again, put on our best clothes, and went to a big dinner down below at the long house. It was a joyous time of thankfulness once again.

So now that Jimmy and I were warm and safe, Lone Buck then took a year's leave of us, which was his way for the next three years. Those were hard years for me, especially the winters. I hiked into aspen groves above my lodge and took down dead standing trees with an axe, then drug or carried the cut sections to my yard and bucked them up with a bow saw or a one-man cross-cut saw. I usually could only do one day's worth of wood in a day as it was extremely hard work. I often dropped into the snow and cried. But I loved the life, and I was so happy that we had our very own home. It was warm and safe; a home for me and my little son. I built a log bed down-stairs and made a bed up in the loft for Jimmy. After supper on a winter's eve we both would crawl into my bed and I read stories to him. Then Jimmy and I would climb the ladder to the loft and I tucked him in. I believe we always said our prayers. I always prayed before bed my whole life. I will always remember my mother's voice as she went off to bed. She would say, "Don't forget to say your prayers".

During the first year on the mountain I had a collapse. I did not understand what was going on inside my body, so I could only relate it to something connected to the years of abuse that I had just came out of. Looking back the symptoms were surely adrenal-related. I had eaten too many sugar cookies as I was baking for Christmas. I bought regular white sugar because I could not afford honey. I guess even then sugar was not agreeable with me. I was stricken with pain over the pancreas area. I became so weakened that I could not get out of bed. I could not do chores or cook for my son. He ate meals at the neighbors and they brought meals to me. They got in my wood and kept fires going. I was down like this for a month. Many of these symptoms are like I have recently experience with adrenal failure. But today I know I cannot eat sugar and even limit the amount of fruit I eat in a day. I have studied extensively and now have a good doctor. I manage this condition as best as one can. But at that time in my life I was not aware of what all my body, mind and spirit had suffered through the abuse of the previous relationship with my son's father. Oh so many lessons in life, and many of them are so hard.

11.
OUR SON WAS BORN

Until I was found with child, Lone Buck spent very little time with us at the homestead on the mountain. Then he was reluctantly bound to me and my little son. He tried to be what he should be to us, but his heart was his own. He never opened up his heart to me. Though he said he loved me, it was not deep. I did not understand this and tried to drag out of him some kind of emotional bond that I could build a foundation on. He could never be more than a big brother to me. He was my superior and I was his subject. That never changed. Once he told me I was his "stuck mate". This was quite a blow to my heart. I was a person who needed love; it was all I ever really wanted all the way back to my childhood. So Buck's indifference and constant absence was very disturbing to me. This is a poem I wrote at that time when I lived in my earth lodge on the mountain where my little son and I were most all the time alone with the other horse people.

Looking to Find

Deep inside my heart there is pain, I've pushed that pain there many times over.

In hopes that, that sunny day would indeed come and wash it away.

Wash it away like the mighty sea washes the old from her shores, and carries it to the universe.

Today I feel like ending my wait for the pain has made me weary.

Today it is not only me who feels the pain, but there is a delicate, tiny new life growing within my belly.

If only I were strong enough to be unaffected by my environment.

To stay high through all those things I let trip me.

But now, today; I am indeed affected. I do feel pain, my head aches, my eyes are swelled with sorrow.

What is it that grieves me so?

"Want", wanting something to be different, wanting to be loved, as I love.

The man whom holds my heart, holds it with hands of confusion.

Does he want my heart; does it sting his hands?

The confusion: I do see its roots; it angers me so often as I see it angers him.

Sometimes I just want to tear my heart away and run.

The Lord tells me that is not the way, so I keep waiting for that sunny day.

Is it myself I see in my man that causes me so much pain?

In similar ways yes; in others no.

He is a mighty man, although weak in some ways.

Ways, opinions that don't flow in the currents of the river.

He tires his mighty trunk as he tries to stand firm in the midst of the flow.

He fights and holds strong to his opinions, to his godly ideals, till he is beaten to exhaustion by the mighty river, the Universe.

Our son was Born

Now in many, many ways he is a wise man, a kind man, giving and swaying, and a beautiful man; if only he could let go of his mighty stand and flow with each bend, and rapid and laziness of the river.

It seems I can see this and it saddens me; it affects my daily life, for the flow of our union was never what he dreamed it would be for him.

He dreamed of beauty, grace, ease, peace of mind; a woman who could predict his every thought, his actions.

Dreams of deep overwhelming love that by conscious choice created his children.

I've failed to live up to any of his dreams.

His child was created through feelings of love but not by conscious choice.

So he punishes himself with dissatisfaction, holding strongly to his godly ideals, allowing the flow of the river to beat him to exhaustion.

This is why I just want to run, to free him because he can't seem to free himself.

It hurts me so to see him so miserable.

I weaken; my hurt turns to anger.

The anger is only my fighting the flow of the river.

I must relax; let the flow carry me away into the universe where I am but a babe in the arms of eternal love.

And as I lay in the arms of love, I too am cradling my babe, within, in the arms of love.

That is what I was chosen to do, I must not let my weakness blur my sight.

I have been chosen to be a mother by the "One", because I am worthy, I am Love, I am strong.

Lone Buck, along with several men from the land, went over to the coast to plant trees in logged areas. His brother lived near where their contract was and so the crew was able to use his house as a base camp, so to speak. Most of the week they camped out on the unit; it was cold and wet in that country. It so happened that my midwife was a man and a tree-planter on the crew. Jimmy and I were left up on the mountain with some of the horse people as one of the husbands was gone on the tree-planting crew.

Up on the mountain we were corralling the horses. We each took a shift leading all the horses and donkeys to the water trough. It was my shift and I was leading a pack donkey named Abraham to the water. After he watered I decided I would jump on his back for a free ride back to the barn. Well, Abraham decided to shorten my ride and that right quick. Instead of following the trail he headed straight down the rather steep hill, bucking all the way. I slid down his neck and landed hard on the ground on my seat. I was hurt badly and pregnant. I drug myself to the nearest lodge. They helped me home and laid me down. At that time I did not know exactly what had happened, but I could hardly move. So I was bed-ridden and my neighbors had to take care of me a lot.

Some of the women knew of a country doctor who made house calls so they reached him. He agreed to come and see me. There was no way I could get to him since we walked to our lodges or traveled on horseback. It was not a climb to be taken lightly; one had to be strong and healthy to make it. I suppose this doctor was strong enough because he made it to my house. He examined me and told me that I had damaged the peripheral nerves in my buttocks and broken my pelvis bone. He ordered strict bed rest for at least a month. I was good to follow his orders. I could do nothing more, I could hardly move. Thank God I had good neighbors to help me.

As the months passed on I healed and was back to caring for myself. But my man Buck was far away working for money. I was very emotional and not feeling much support or love from him. He never was good to write many letters: a few in a years' time. But now I was carrying his child I thought things would change. They really did not. I was sad and lonely for him. I cried a lot and wrote letters to him.

I went to a women's clinic in town for a few checkups to make sure I was doing well and the baby was strong. As I was around six months I saw a doctor. He did an ultra sound and reported all was well. I was on vitamins and eating healthy foods. My diet was basically vegetarian. I was strong in my body; it was just my heart that was broken.

When I was about seven and a half months along I decided I would take Jimmy and go to be near the tree- planters, both Buck and my midwife (husband). We, of course, stayed in Buck's brothers' house. It was comfortable and had a bath tub. Ahhh, I could soak my aching back in hot water every day! For many years all we had for a bathtub was a galvanized wash tub, to which I carried all the water for from the well, then heating it on the wood stove. Jimmy and I used the same water to save on time and labor. This hot running water in a tub that I could lay down in was delightful.

The men only came home on weekends and occasionally when they switched units and had a day's break, so I did not see Buck or my midwife very often. And when I did the men were busy with tree planting business, so they paid very little attention to me.

When they were gone I spent a lot of time walking. It was spring, the grass was green, and the flowers were blooming. It was lovely there but it rained a lot.

My stomach was constantly plagued with heartburn and I needed milk to put the fire out. At home we bought milk from a family that milked cows and goats. They delivered to the land all the things that they made. So I drank Jersey milk with the cream on, at least some of it. We brought the cheese, yogurt, milk, and butter up the mountain in panniers, which are large saddle bags made solely for packing; on the horse or donkey. I liked to ride my horse so I tied the dairy products on to the saddle in saddle bags or burlap bags. I really could not do without the milk because my stomach burned all the time. So when I arrived at Buck's brother's place I sought out a cow. And indeed I found a Jersey cow about a mile up the road. So I bought milk from them, but I had to walk there and carry it home. This was not so good for my back, which was still suffering from my fall, not to mention, that by then I was very pregnant. Jimmy helped; he could carry one gallon.

Sometimes Jimmy went with Buck to the unit to be water-boy. So then the house was very quiet. Buck's brother had a girl roommate, the only other woman around. But she really wasn't there very much. She worked and went to college. And I don't even remember her coming home every evening. I rarely saw her.

Finally I was nearing my due date and still the crew just simply wasn't around. I so longed for an encouraging word, a back rub or a bit of sympathy. Then one evening they pulled in and Buck informed me that it was time to have the baby because they had three days off. That night I went into labor after 'the crew' was all snoring. I knew they were tired so I did not wake anyone until I was starting to have hard labor. You see the tree- planting crew was also the birthing crew. There was my midwife, Buck's brother, the other man from the horse people and Jimmy. Jimmy was not there the whole time; he waited downstairs 'till the baby was born. Each had an assignment: one was the camera man and Buck, of course, was the one to tune into me up front. The midwife gave the orders and was to catch the baby. So when I finally alerted the crew the house began to buzz. The man from the horse people was well-versed in delivering babies: all his were birthed at home. His wife was strong, vibrant and healthy. They had beautiful children.

So my pains increased in strength as the night progressed. I had to birth on my hands and knees to avoid back labor because of the many accidents I had had in my life that affected my low back. So when a contraction started, Buck supported my upper body so I could put all my strength into the contraction. I was quite vocal. I think this helped me whether anyone else thought so or not. I think all the dogs in the neighborhood were howling with me. Then just before the dawn my baby boy was born. He came out in the sack intact. There is something special about this and special indeed was this baby boy. I think that it is said that one born in the sack would be a prophet or man of God. The midwife quickly broke the sack so he could breathe. He had the cord around his neck but not too tightly, he was okay. The midwife rapidly took care of it. All was well and they laid my baby on my chest. It was a beautiful night. Soon with our son wrapped in swaddling clothes, Buck walked with him in the room while I birthed the placenta. The work was done and I was so tired. The crew cleaned up the mess and left our little family to bask in awe as the night turned to dawn. All was well.

12.

ALWAYS WAITING

We stayed on there for a month or more until tree-planting was over. During that time we tried and tried to think of a name for our son, wanting to get to know him a bit before we gave him a name. Buck decided to name him after two of his grandfathers, taking the names and combining them. So our son was called Lewis Carl. I'll call him Lew for short. He was a good baby, nursed strongly and grew in leaps and bounds. I swaddled him most of the time and he simply was at peace. He slept quite well through most of the night within the first week. I had to alter my diet a bit and cut out things like garlic and so much rich Jersey milk. My stomach stopped hurting so much as soon as Lew was born, so that was workable. I loved my baby boy and was so glad to see him face to face and sing to him songs of love.

While we waited for the planting contracts to be completed, the men were home on a weekend and Buck's brother had a friend drop by for a visit. We were all in the living room visiting with this man. He evidently was some type of medium or someone who talked with spirits. He used an Ouija board to reach these spirits. It appeared to me that the man was contacting good spirits or angels, or so I thought in my ignorance.

He began to tell us all about our past lives and how some of us knew each other in previous life times. This kind of belief was never my own and it was my experience as a child that Ouija boards only contacted demons. I was afraid of those spirits of which I had, had bad experiences when I was in my early teens and got into some of those devilish activities. But I am gullible and was somewhat taken in to some of these visions this man was seeing.

Soon we were all home again as a whole family and it felt so good. Buck found work locally and did not leave us alone as in previous years. But he was gone long days. He purchased a 4x4 pick up and was determined now to drive to the lodge instead of walk from down below. This presented its problems once the snow came. We rigged a V plow and tried to keep the field road open. This worked some of the time. Buck had to chain up all four wheels before coming up the mountain. He usually stopped at the tavern and had a few beers before coming home and this just added to the hours away from home. We often were all in bed before he arrived. I remember lying in bed looking out the loft window, which now was built over the whole floor below, toward the little town where the tavern was and watched the car lights come and go. I could see if they came out our road or not. If they did I would gauge how long it would take him to get to the yard. But more often than not he just did not come and then I watched for another set of headlights to see if these might be his. It seems I spent most of my life waiting for him. He was famous for being late or just not showing up. The worst of it was that he was usually somewhat drunk. This was offensive to me because of my last relationship when I would be beaten regularly by a drunken man. I tried to plead with him not to stop at the tavern, or to limit his intake to one beer, but he was a wimp when his friends would keep offering to buy him one more. He would totally miss seeing the children, for they were asleep when he got home and asleep when he left before dawn. I could never reach him, ever.

My days at home were full of hard work, but not as hard as when I had to bring the fire wood down out of the mountains by myself. Now the wood was stacked in a shed out back of the lodge. My hardest task now was carrying the water up from the well. I used a yoke that a friend gave me to lessen my labor. The yoke was a hollowed-out log that perfectly fit over my shoulders and made a U around my neck. It was about four feet long and I attached hooks on each end to hook on to five gallon buckets. I filled them full at the well, where we dropped a well bucket down into the water and drew it up on a rope and pulley. The well was hand dug by us horse people and kept squeaky clean by us horsey ladies. When need be we would siphon out the water and one of us climbed down a ladder and the other one was on top with a bucket to lower down and pull back up. We scooped out everything off the bottom and put it into the bucket and the lady on the top pulled it out and dumped it. We scrubbed the bottom, which was solid rock and then bleached it. Then we were done. It was essential to have two at this job. So then back to laundry day, I carried my full buckets of water to the lodge uphill from the well. Those buckets full, weighed eighty pounds and I was only about one hundred five pounds, so this was hard work for me. I had to chop cook stove wood to heat the water and then I would scrub my diapers and baby clothes in a wash tub. Sometimes I used a scrub board. I had a glass one, which is easier on your knuckles, or I used a plunger, which was designed especially for washing clothes. I did not do all of our clothes this way; mostly baby things or light things that were needed. We went to the laundromat occasionally. I had a clothes line outdoors and I loved hanging out clothes. In the winter they would freeze like a board so I put up ropes in the rafters to dry clothes in the lodge.

Most of my work revolved around the children: preparing meals and keeping every one well-clothed. I liked to sew things for the boys. One time I made this really warm coat of wool for Jimmy, but he never wore it because it was so thick he couldn't move. I made it all by hand. Oh well.

   My relationship with Buck never seemed to improve even though I tried hard to talk things out and come to a common bond. But things were quite lop-sided. This was a constant weight on my heart; a sadness that never went away. Maybe momentarily; things were not always sad. There were lots of good times and I felt Buck's love in as much as he was able to love me. We could talk about everyday things and we had a lot in common. I guess what I'm trying to describe is a depth, a oneness that is supposed to be between a man and wife. But we weren't married and neither of us knew God personally. We both prayed to God, or who we thought God was. But could He hear our prayers when we were living in sin and forsaking His law, His Way, and His only Son? Maybe what my heart longed for was that love that only God can give and I wanted it from this man that could not give it to me.

13.
WE BOUGHT A COW

As the boys grew I felt we needed to produce our own milk and I proposed buying a cow. We knew a farmer who had one for sale; it had a little beef blood in it and would produce nice butcher steers. Buck agreed this would be good. It is obvious that one needs a barn to have a milk cow so I made a plan for a 16'x 16' pole barn. For this I got no support. I was a pretty determined person, and industrious, so I set out to accomplish this alone. I started with good-sized timbers from green trees. I was still on my own with this project, so I set out to the forest with an axe and chopped down appropriate-sized trees for the barn. I had trained my saddle horse to skid logs; therefore I went after them with my horse. I had a logging harness for her and we were in business. Once to the barn site I stripped them and began construction. I got the whole structure up by myself except the ridge pole with which I did get Buck to help, along with one of the neighbors. I divided the barn down the center with a partition and then divided half of it into quarters. One quarter was for the hay and one quarter was for the calf. I built a box to hold a twenty gallon water trough that extended into the calf stall and the cow stall. I packed it in with saw dust. In the cow stall was a feeder and a stanchion. The farmer with the cow patiently waited for me to finish this work and then sold us the cow. I was in hog heaven, but not Buck. He was the baby sitter while I was doing all this and he was feeling jealous, I guess. So it was a bit of contention between us. But when the milk began to flow it was a rich feeling to serve all the milk we could drink, along with cottage cheese with cream poured over the top. I made hard cheese and butter, too. It was a blessing. It was easy keeping the milk cold in the winter but the summer came and we had to lower a stainless steel can down into the well water. It was delightful to draw up the can and drink a jar of ice cold milk on a hot day.

14.
I LEFT THE MOUNTAIN

With this hot dry summer the well dried up. That spring the men plowed us a big garden plot near the barn, which was on a bench below the lodge. We intended to get a gravity feed line going to the garden from the well. They used the neighbors' draft horse and plow to turn over the sod. Then I came along with my saddle horse hitched to a stone boat and I gathered all the sod off and piled it on the perimeters. It was a nice garden and the soil was rich. We planted but it never took off because our water supply diminished to the point that there was only house water left for the three homesteads that were on the mountain. By the end of summer there was no water. We were hauling it up in fifty five gallon drums on the pickup from the spring down below. That worked for house water, but not for keeping a garden alive. Not to mention we were watering cows and horses. Life began to get harder and tension was building. Then winter came and snow. We really depended on that truck making it up the mountain with water. Buck was pushing it hard, and with the short winter days he was bringing water up after work. It was dark and cold. Of course he had to chain up all fours before coming up the mountain. This means lying in the cold snow, in the dark, and fumbling with the chains. I would be down doing chores listening for the whine of the 4x4 in low range topping the hill and headin' for home. Buck would pull up close to the lodge and we would do the bucket relay to an empty barrel indoors near the stove. By this time he had built on an addition to the east side of the lodge. This broadened our living area and we even had a kitchen table to eat at. This is where the wood heat stove was now located. The water barrel next to it stayed warm. I had a large cook stove in the center of the original house.

I liked to keep a twelve hour interval between milkings so I was up early in the dark of winter and ready to head to the barn about 6:30a.m. I carried warm water in five gallon buckets on my yoke, then a milk bucket and wash bucket in one hand and in the other I carried red glowing hot grates, which I kept in the stove all night to get hot. They were grates of iron from the inside of an old cook stove. I made wire loops through holes that were in them. I carried them with a hay hook. So with all this I slipped and skidded down the trail to the barn. Sometimes I crashed in the snow and cried. Upon arriving at the barn I put the red hot grates in the water trough to melt the ice and warm the cow's water, then adding the warm water from the house. In spite of the hard work I loved the cows and I loved milking. My cow loved me, too; she would lick my face and my fur hat with her sand paper tongue. Often in the evenings when it was dark and the snow was so deep, it would be exhausting just to make it back to the lodge. Jimmy was old enough to keep an eye on Lew if dad was not home yet. The barn was only a holler away but there was a steep hill to climb. Deep snow makes the going tough.

One night as I was at the barn waiting to hear the 4x4 coming with the water for the cows, I heard the engine whining, then it came to a screeching halt. When Buck came walking up without the truck he informed me that he dropped the drive line in the snow. We were sunk. This was not the first time or the last that we would kill the drive line in this truck which Dad called the "Iron Horse". Well this just meant that he would be lying under the truck soon in the snow fixing the drive line. He would miss work until it was fixed. The cows had to have water, so we sledded buckets from the truck. It was a hard winter. And it was obvious that we could not live on the mountain, and milk cows without a well.

Buck and I were not getting along very well. I could not bear it any longer. Lew was two and when spring had come I decided to take the children, the cows and my horses, and make my abode down below near the water where you could get to the plowed road easily. I moved into an old school bus and took out a bank loan to build a house barn combination. Some of the other horse people had moved down and had their horses and barbwire fences. It was accepted. Seven years had passed since we first settled here and reality was sinking in. The people were not as idealistic. My hope was to make cheese and sell milk enough to support the children and me. So I did the fencing, put up a lean-to for the cow, and had a carpenter start the house barn. It towered into sky. I was happy to be out of the stress of living with a man who was miserable with me and our life. He, too, was glad and seemed to be indifferent to me and the children. When I left he tore down my barn.

Lew became sick with what us women decided was the measles. He was very sick with a high fever. There were a few of us women who were doctoring him. We put up curtains to keep out the light and were giving him herbs to help the fever break and put him into a sweat. I was worried and sent word up to Buck to bring down some herbs I had in the lodge. He never responded to us or even let us know he cared. Us women pulled together our resources and things went as well as could be expected. He sweated out his fever and it did break. There never seemed to be any setbacks or ill effects from the fever.

Then a man from town began to take an interest in me, and when Buck saw this, he changed his mind and wanted the family to be back together. So that happened and we all lived in the bus. It was a happy reunion. There still was no water in the well on the mountain. It just was not an option to live up there anymore. Living down below made it easy for Jimmy to get on the school bus as it stopped just a holler away from the bus that we were living in. It was hard for him when we lived up there on the mountain. It was an hour's hike coming up after school on snowy nights in the winter. It was not that he wasn't used to the hike, he did it all the time by choice to play with his best friend, but to do it after school was tough. I had a baby at home so I could not go after him on the horse very often unless I left the baby with the neighbors or with Dad if he was home. If it was extra cold I went after him, but one stayed warmer walking than riding. Nevertheless I did not want him out there in the cold alone. He was tough and healthy and wore appropriate clothing, though I think he was teased at school because of his boots and such, but he had to have them and he wore them in spite of teasing. The first year he went to school from home was third grade. I taught him at home through first grade. And I thought him too young yet to walk the mountain daily to the bus stop, so I had him go stay with Granma and Granpa for his second year. This was good for him and he made good grades. He is very intelligent beyond his years. He loved his Grandparents and they loved him. We lived with them when he was a baby so they were very attached to him.

15.

BORN AGAIN

Under the circumstances, we were contemplating moving to another state and leaving our friends behind. We took a trip to scout out an area we were interested in, inquiring about logging in the area. That was what Buck wanted to do for a living. He was good at it and loved the woods. The climate was much warmer where we wanted to go. I was open to it if this was the right thing to do. Leaving our friends would be hard, though.

When we got home I was torn about the move and wanted to know what God wanted for our lives. But at this point I did not really know God, though I prayed often I had never come to a personal relationship with Him, and I was living in sin. One day I was at a yard sale and what did I see but an Ouija board. I thought this is how I will contact some of God's angels and ask what we should do. So I bought it and went home. But I needed another person to make it work. So I asked my friend to assist in this quest, and she agreed. So we began to ask whether we should make this move, I don't remember if the spirit we contacted answered that question but it began to tell us of our past connections with these people in previous life times. The spirit told us its name and then began to tell us things we did not ask. This spirit became so aggressive that it spoke in an audible voice through my friend. We really hardly needed the board. It told us that the police were planning a raid on the community where we lived; a drug raid. Well, as mothers this was a huge concern; we were not growing anything illegal, but others there were. We were told by this spirit that our land would be confiscated and all of us would lose our homes and everything we had worked so hard to accomplish there. We were horrified because we knew for sure there was a spirit speaking to us. We were convinced it was a good spirit. So we informed our men folk of this thing and got them into our fear. They came and listened to the spirit for themselves and went along with a plan to save our homes and families. We must extinguish the plants. This spirit told us the police would come by 6:00a.m. So as night was falling we all went in different directions to notify the residents. That night there was a field-burning and many a house-cleaning.

We were up all night and when 6:00a.m. arrived, no police came. We went to the spirit and it told us there was a forest fire that delayed their coming. 7:00a.m. came and no police. Then 8:00a.m. came and still no police. My friend and I were beside ourselves and we all were highly charged with anxiety. We were down near our bus when some of the residents came and were very mad. Buck was so mad that he punched his truck. His highly respectable position had just been put in the dirt. Now he was mad magnified; he had broken his right hand, so off to the ER for a cast. This was not a good day. And it was all my fault! My friend and I got together to talk alone. She was so convinced this spirit was telling us the truth, it was actually speaking through her. But by this time I was convinced that it was an evil spirit of the devil and it was playing tricks on us. So we each took different paths from that day forward. She and her man had a nice home and they did not want to leave there, so opted to wade through the turmoil of the anger of all who lived there. Buck and I were wantin' to move anyway, so we did, but just to the surrounding area. We rented a farm house. He got on a logging crew and I was to do some farm labor as part of our rental agreement. We were right on the highway and Jimmy could get on the bus from our driveway. This was a very good move for us. We had all the modern conveniences, especially a bathtub! Buck had work and we could start a new life together. The house was an old two-storied farm house. The barn was huge and about three stories; it had milking stanchions and a large area with feed bunks. I was in hog heaven! We butchered our old cows and purchased a Guernsey that was milking so we had lots of cream. I was making cheese, butter and yogurt. We had a large kitchen and dining table. We loved it there, but were only able to stay about a year as the ranchers went bankrupt.

During this time on the ranch I was searching for God. I really was confused because all I ever had known was deception. All the years I spent surrounded by new age thinkers had its influence on my thinking. Buck was inclined after a Hindu sort of philosophy. Many friends were into fairies and nature spirits; some were into the Indian idea of the Great Spirit. Some had gurus and others had medicine men and some had shamans. My head was spinning. All I knew was that what I had done to contact what I thought was a "good spirit" was in actuality a demon. I had been raised to believe that God manifested Himself in three persons; the Father, Son and Holy Ghost. I still believed this and I always prayed this way, but somehow that belief had been clouded in the many influences that I had lived among. So in this time I was engulfed in confusion and despair. I cried myself to sleep at night and pleaded with God to show me how to find Him.

We moved into another house not far away. It too, was very convenient for Jimmy to get on the school bus. We also had close neighbors with a little boy about his age. We lived there for the school year, and it was then that I finally got an answer to my question to God, "How do I find you?" One day He answered me in something like an audible voice and said, "My Son". Well of course I knew that Jesus was God's Son and this was what I needed to hear. My search for other gods was over. I was now certain which direction to go, but the problem was that I went to another book beside the Bible to learn about Jesus. This book was portraying Him as something less than the only begotten Son of God. It conveyed that His death on the cross for the forgiveness of sins was some barbaric myth. And since He was portrayed as something less than God incarnate there was no resurrection. I sunk myself into this book and then I was confused once again.

Buck's mother was a Christian and was led of God one day to call me on the phone. She just asked me if I wanted to pray the sinners' prayer with her and I said, "Yes!" So I got down on my knees and repeated the prayer and meant it with all my heart, confessing my faith in the Son of God, Jesus Christ, and what He did on the cross to save sinners like me, accepting Him as my Lord and Saviour. When I stood up I was "born again", a new creature in Christ. I was so happy. But my confusion was not gone yet as I kept reading that deceptive book. God was patient with me.

Now that I had the indwelling of God's own Spirit I began to develop conviction. I changed some of my habits. I knew that very day when God entered my heart that I could no longer smoke weed in my corn cob pipe, my life was now His. I no longer continued with my dance group, which consisted of women with many strange gods. And I knew that I could no longer just live with Buck; we had to be married. But I did not know the scriptures that say that a Christian is to marry, "only in the Lord", so early that summer we planned to marry.

When we still were living on the land we had begun to invest in a parcel of our own along a creek not far away. So at this time we wanted to develop it rather than to keep spending money on rent. This we did. We dug a well upstream, laid pipe, and got gravity feed water to our house site and barn. We purchased an older small mobile home and set it up, put in a corral for the horses and began fencing. By summer we were ready to move in and get married. Our wedding ceremony was there on our place. It was beautiful. I made my own wedding dress, which was a teal green. It had a very full skirt. I rode my white horse to the altar. She had red peonies in her tail. My skirt draped over her whole back. We were happy to be married. We decided to go back to our given names, mine being Belinda and his Gabriel. Now I was called by his last name legally: Belinda Decker.

Life continued as before the wedding. Gabriel was starting a new logging job the next day. The children and I were off on a Greyhound bus to visit my parents. We did not go on a honeymoon. It would have been good, I think, but we were poor and Gabriel's job was starting. He needed a good steady job. At my folks' we had a little wedding reception with cake and punch. That way they sorta took part in our wedding and sent gifts home with me.

16.

MY NEW FAITH

I met a Christian family. They were trying to persuade me to read only the Bible and throw that other book away that I had been reading. So one day as I prayed for the Lord to show me the truth and help me understand the blood He shed on the cross, these scriptures came to me that morning as I sat beside the wood stove in my rocking chair.

> **John 6:47-63** Verily, verily, I say unto you, He that believeth on me hath everlasting life. I am that bread of life. Your fathers did eat manna in the wilderness, and are dead. This is the bread which cometh down from heaven, that a man may eat thereof, and not die. I am the living bread which came down from heaven: if any man eat of this bread, he shall live for ever: and the bread that I will give is my flesh, which I will give for the life of the world. The Jews therefore strove among themselves, saying, How can this man give us *his* flesh to eat? Then Jesus said unto them, Verily, verily, I say unto you, Except ye eat the flesh of the Son of man, and drink his blood, ye have no life in you. Whoso eateth my flesh, and drinketh my blood, hath eternal life; and

> I will raise him up at the last day. For my flesh is meat indeed, and my blood is drink indeed. He that eateth my flesh, and drinketh my blood, dwelleth in me, and I in him. As the living Father hath sent me, and I live by the Father: so he that eateth me, even he shall live by me. This is that bread which came down from heaven: not as your fathers did eat manna, and are dead: he that eateth of this bread shall live for ever. These things said he in the synagogue, as he taught in Capernaum. Many therefore of his disciples, when they had heard *this*, said, This is an hard saying; who can hear it? When Jesus knew in himself that his disciples murmured at it, he said unto them, Doth this offend you? *What* and if ye shall see the Son of man ascend up where he was before? It is the spirit that quickeneth; the flesh profiteth nothing: the words that I speak unto you, *they* are spirit, and *they* are life.

I knew then that once again I had been deceived in to believing a lie so I went at once and threw that other deceptive book away. From that day forward I read only the Bible, the Word of God.

Because of my new faith in Christ, I was a festering thorn in my husband's flesh. My view of truth conflicted with his and his way of comforting himself was by insulting me with sarcastic remarks constantly. Then there was conflict between the boys; it made for an uncomfortable and unhappy home.

One day Gabriel and I got into a spat. I jumped into my car and headed into the little town a few miles down the road. I went into the store and bought me a quart of dark beer. I commenced to drinking it. I was by myself standing on the street when I heard the Lord's voice speak to me. He said very clearly, "Why do you not come to me for your comfort?" Yes, I was denying Him by drinking that beer instead of trusting Him to comfort me in my sadness. I turned that beer upside

My New Faith

down right there on the street, poured out every drop, and trashed the bottle. From that day forward I never touched a drop of alcohol.

Gabriel was gone logging for the whole week and only came home on weekends. He was tired and did not appreciate the turmoil at home. So there was trouble. His verbal assaults were constant. He was not happy or content so we all took the brunt of his discontent. Mostly it was upon Jimmy and me, but sometimes Lew as well. I could not tolerate any physical abuse toward the children.

One Saturday morning after he had returned from the logging unit, I had asked him to have a talk with the boys about their fighting. He took Jimmy outside and was very rough with him; he picked him up and slammed him against the trailer. Then he came inside and grabbed Lew and began to shake him. I could not tolerate this abuse any longer. I stood up, confronted him, and threw my coffee cup at him to stop him from hurting the boys. Then he grabbed me by my shoulders, picked me clean off the ground, and slammed me against the wall. There were nails hammered in the wall to hang coats on and one sliced open my shoulder. I was bleeding. It was a gaping wound. I was so traumatized that I ran out of the house and did not come back for three days. I went to a friend's house that lived alone and she did not tell anyone where I was. She treated my wounds. I did not see a doctor, but probably needed stitches. I still have the scar today.

Buck never came looking for me or even cared where I was. When I finally came home he did not even ask where I had been. Never an apology for what he did to me, though he did apologize to Jimmy for being so rough with him. My heart was broken, fore I loved him. I tried desperately to talk these things out but he would not hear me.

I kept my focus on Jesus and as I really did not know the Bible well, there was one verse I kept referring to and that was, **Romans 12:17** Recompense to no man evil for evil. So I took all the verbal blows in silence, but inside I was mortally wounded. I felt like a wild animal in a cage huddled in the corner to protect myself from the blows of my master.

Sometime later I met a teenage girl named Brea who was coming down the mountain on horseback to a neighboring farm to buy grain; her family was milking a cow. I had broke a mule for that farmer and she was putting some riding hours on him. So I ran into her quite often. I found her intriguing because she wore a kerchief and a long skirt and she was really good with horses. She and her family were Christians. She invited me to come up to meet her mother and siblings. So I rode my horse up there. Drew was on back of my saddle. They had a child about his age. It was a nice day. I had lots of questions, but the mother, Mrs. Mullin was not answering me. She kept saying I would have to ask her husband, who was away with their oldest son working. She expected them back in a few weeks. This seemed strange to me and I sensed fear in her. So I continued to see Brea out on the trail occasionally and we visited. I liked her a lot. Soon she told me her father was home and he brought gifts. Her gift was a pistol that she was to carry when she was out riding. So we planned a day when I could come up, meet him and ask my questions.

I was a new Christian and I really was only learning the Bible, but in spite of this I did know the New Testament fairly well and because of this I was able to discern, eventually. I went up on an afternoon in late fall. They had prepared a picnic for me and my son, Lew. They laid out a blanket with food. It was a lovely spot near a grove of aspens. But for me it was rather cold and soon I was shivering. Mr. Mullin was talking to me and to me only. He could hardly be interrupted and I don't even remember asking many questions. Finally it was getting toward evening. We moved indoors and all sat around a long table. I was impressed how the younger children sat silent and barely moved. Then the women, Mrs. Mullin and Brea, served a supper meal. I was on one end of the table and Mr. Mullin, was at the other end. He demanded my rapt attention so that I could scarcely eat my meal. In all his discourse the thing that impressed me the most was that he kept repeating that he was without sin. This was disturbing to me because I know that no man is without sin. His eyes were evil-looking and he wore a cap, even in the house, which had an emblem on it of a bull with red wicked eyes and blood on its horns. It was quite fitting to the person of the man. He certainly did not give me the impression of a man of God. Finally it was getting late. Lew and I had to be going. I hinted of this over and over, but was not allowed to excuse myself from this one-sided conversation. Eventually I made our exit. Brea drove us down the mountain in a truck. There my car was parked.

A few days later Brea and I drove together to look at some goats that were for sale and on our return home we drove past a lake. There was her father baptizing a few adults of the family that lived at the bottom of the road that led to their place. These folks, the Gillahans, were not well-versed in the Bible, but were sincere in wanting to be Christians.

Brea asked me to stop. So we did, got out and joined in. I was asked if I had been baptized. I had been as an infant and then again by my little sister, who was not a minister, neither at that time was I "born again". So Mr. Mullin assured me I needed to be baptized properly. I was not feeling comfortable but I consented. I watched the others go first. It was a cold day and the lake had begun to freeze. They had to break the ice. I had no extra clothing to change into. I was not feeling comfortable and I was actually pacing back and forth like an animal in a cage. But I am gullible and too often allow people to take advantage of me. And this was a prime example. So it came my turn and I allowed Mr. Mullin to baptize me. He claimed to be an ordained minister. After the baptism we quickly left; I was freezing. I dropped Brea off at her

Deliverance from Oppression

road and went home, where I explained to my husband what happened. He did not say much, but I could tell he was displeased.

The next day was Sunday and I had been invited to come up to the Mullin's for a service and communion, along with the Gillahan family. The Lord was giving me scriptures and I was certain this man was not of God, but was on a power quest and literally held his family in fearful captivity. I had only one intention and that was to present Mr. Mullin with the scriptures and leave. My little son, Lew, was with me. Again Brea met me and the Gillahan family at the bottom of the mountain to drive us up in her truck. When we arrived everyone went in to be seated at the long table, but I went first to visit the bushes. So when I came in, all were seated, including Lew. They saved me a seat right next to Mr. Mullin. I was not comfortable, but God made me strong. I wasted no time in presenting these scriptures.

> **1 John 1:5-10** This then is the message which we have heard of him, and declare unto you, that God is light, and in him is no darkness at all. If we say that we have fellowship with him, and walk in darkness, we lie, and do not the truth: But if we walk in the light, as he is in the light, we have fellowship one with another, and the blood of Jesus Christ his Son cleanseth us from all sin. If we say that we have no sin, we deceive ourselves, and the truth is not in us. If we confess our sins, he is faithful and just to forgive us *our* sins, and to cleanse us from all unrighteousness. If we say that we have not sinned, we make him a liar, and his word is not in us. **1 John 2:1-2** My little children, these things write I unto you, that ye sin not. And if any man sin, we have an advocate with the Father, Jesus Christ the righteous: And he is the propitiation for our sins: and not for ours only, but also for *the sins of* the whole world.

My New Faith

Romans 3:9-23 What then? are we better *than they*? No, in no wise: for we have before proved both Jews and Gentiles, that they are all under sin; As it is written, There is none righteous, no, not one: There is none that understandeth, there is none that seeketh after God. They are all gone out of the way, they are together become unprofitable; there is none that doeth good, no, not one. Their throat *is* an open sepulchre; with their tongues they have used deceit; the poison of asps *is* under their lips: Whose mouth *is* full of cursing and bitterness: Their feet *are* swift to shed blood: Destruction and misery *are* in their ways: And the way of peace have they not known: There is no fear of God before their eyes. Now we know that what things soever the law saith, it saith to them who are under the law: that every mouth may be stopped, and all the world may become guilty before God. Therefore by the deeds of the law there shall no flesh be justified in his sight: for by the law *is* the knowledge of sin. But now the righteousness of God without the law is manifested, being witnessed by the law and the prophets; Even the righteousness of God *which is* by faith of Jesus Christ unto all and upon all them that believe: for there is no difference: For all have sinned, and come short of the glory of God;

This did not go over well. He slammed his fist on the table and yelled, "How dare you to contradict me in my own house and before my family!" Well, I had said what I needed to say, so I quickly stood up and motioned to Lew. We both got out of there and ran. Brea came running after us. She was crying and tried to assure us that we needed to come back. But I was done. I could clearly see that this man was a power monger and very dangerous. His family was his victims. She drove us down the mountain.

I went home and told Gabriel. He was not happy. I understood, but I felt I had to say what I did for the sake of Mr. Mullin's victims. Soon the Gillahans that were there at the table showed up at our house. They came in to tell us they too were not feeling comfortable with the whole scene. They had picked up on my unrest at the baptism when I was pacing back and forth. They left after me and in agreement with me, so the scene was heated. This excitement filled our house and my husband.

Soon there was trouble between the Mullins on the top of the mountain and the Gillahans on the bottom. We saw from our yard that the sheriff actually came because the Gillahans at the bottom were being threatened. Somebody put nails on the road.

I stayed away from them and was sorry for my friend Brea. She was entrapped. The story goes on. I am thankful I did what I did because it must have enlightened Brea. She met a young man over the fence of a neighboring farm where he was employed. They fell in love. This all took place in the absence of her father as he was gone a lot of the time. When he found out he forbade her to see this boy. But in his absence she eloped with him and went into hiding. I heard later that the father found them and took them into his control again. I may not have the whole story but that is the jist of it.

A later report from a hunter who once looked down on the Mullin's farm saw several women working in Mr. Mullin's garden. They were all dressed in long skirts and kerchiefs. He was walking among them, but not working. There were other men, too, but it appeared that they, too, were under the control of this man, Mr. Mullin. There were rumors about all this; how much is true is unknown.

In time they moved off the mountain and were gone from our lives.

This incident only added fuel to my husband's attitude toward me and therefore his attacks were more insulting than ever. I began to cling to a family of real Christians, the Willards, the ones whom I had mentioned persuaded me to stop reading that other book about a fictitious Jesus, and read only the Bible. One night I stayed the night at their cabin way up on a mountain in our area. I don't remember: why I stayed the night but this I remember. I lay upon the bed that I was given, and I think I was startled from a bad dream. As I turned to look out the window, I saw a red-eyed demon slinking away from me, defeated. I, of course, prayed God for protection and He was there guarding me. That demon could not touch me. The next day I discussed it with the Willards and they told me they thought it was because I had not succumbed to the control of that demonic man, Mr. Mullin, but rather exposed him to all. The devil was no doubt spittin' mad.

Things only worsened with my husband and me. I was attending a church in the valley and, though I did not condemn or preach to Gabriel, I did ask him to come with us to church. He always declined; this was the church of the pastor that had performed our wedding. I recall that once Gabriel did consent to a family photo for the church directory. I don't think he ever came to a service unless possibly on Christmas. So I went with the children without him. This only caused more separation between us. There was a battle of the spirits in our home.

I did not even know what Post Traumatic Stress Disorder was, but I was diagnosed later, resulting from the previous relationship with Jimmy's father. My ability to cope was impaired. Though I endured this abuse for years, it was completely damaging to my inner man. Why does a person go on in this type of situation? I suppose it is a value on the family institution that fuels our endurance. I tried to get my husband to go to counseling, but he would not because in his own eyes he had no fault. Finally I asked the pastor to come to our house and speak with him. The pastor came one day but got nowhere. Gabriel would not discuss his problem with me or with a pastor. And, oh, so often I called a counsel between us to try and resolve our problems. Never could I suggest that there was something that he needed to see and change. Always in all the troubles I was the one to blame and was given long lectures, which I sat through silently. I tried to make myself better and apply that which I could to my life. But changes in me never countered the fiery darts that he threw at my heart.

Finally I had come to the point where I as a person could not exist under this kind of emotional oppression. I walked out on my husband. He was so hurt that I would do this, but yet he refused to discuss it. He would not allow me to take our son, Lew. I never intended to leave him behind; he wanted to be with me. We had never been separated a day in our lives. That was a traumatic day.

17.
FINDING THE MENNONITES

I had previously gotten a waitress job, my first job in ten years. It was important to me to stay home and be a mother to my children. Gabriel was between jobs so I had taken the opportunity to get employment. Therefore, I had the money to rent a small mobile home in town. So this was where I went that woeful day I left my husband.

Soon it was necessary to keep my younger son, Lew, as his dad was working long hours. The boys could get on the school bus right outside the house. So I was blessed to be with my son again. The turmoil between the boys continued. I tried to settle matters and discipline the boys. I, too, was in the middle of the strife. Jimmy was a teen-ager and too big for spankings, so grounding was my mode of discipline. He was addicted to the Nintendo. To take it away was like cutting off an arm. I asked our pastor to get involved and he shook us off like we didn't exist.

Life was hard. I was working full time and going to night school to get my GED. I remember there being piles of dirty dishes. We all pitched in to keep things together, so we took turns in the dish-washing department. Our landlords were right next door, about a stone throw away. We lived right along the river. It was an old farmstead. The landlords were elderly. They owned a milk cow, but could hardly milk her. So I took on the milking, which I loved. This cow had lots of cream, so I made cheese, yogurt and butter. I remember the cheese press rigged up in the middle of the kitchen floor. We had electricity and a refrigerator for the first time since my older boy was a baby. This made life easier and was wonderful for keeping the milk cold.

After a year I was discontented with the area churches I had attended in the valley. I saw so many discrepancies between the people and what the Bible taught. Another family, the Barkers, that I had become friends with also felt the same way. So as a team Mrs. Barker and I set out on a journey to find a church that lived by the Bible. We had been told there was a Mennonite church in the next state, so we put that town on our route. We stopped in all the little towns along the way, interviewed ministers and checked unemployment offices for jobs. But as we did not find anything impressive, we found ourselves in the town where the Mennonites lived. We observed their families at the grocery store and were impressed. It seemed at the time that we were being led to this people. We contacted their ministers and asked for literature, which they mailed to our home town. So with this we ended our search and went home the next day to read about what they believed.

That night we got a hotel in town and were just bedding down when we heard screaming in one of the rooms near ours. Then we heard a man's voice yelling and a lot of crashing and bashing. I told Mrs. Barker I was going to see what was happening. She warned me not to go lest I get hurt also. But I just could not stand by while a woman was being beat up. I had experienced this too many times myself to do nothing. So I got dressed. It was a chilly night. I went, stood outside and listened to the screaming and yelling, soon the door opened and one or the other person was flying out the door. I knew there was nothing I could do physically to stop this man from beating the woman, but I was praying.

Then I was compelled to go stand beside the open door to their room. This immediately stopped the man from hitting her. He mocked me and she began to speak to me. My companion, Mrs. Barker, called the management, they came down there, had a conversation with the man, who evidently he had been drinking, and they threatened to call the police. In the meantime the woman and I discussed her options for escape. She had no money to get away from her boyfriend, but wanted to. She had a relative in another state where she could go. I told her we would try to get her a bus ticket to get her out of there the next morning. The manager separated them for the night and we called a church to get a donation. We took her to a bus the next morning and she escaped her abusive boyfriend. We prayed for her to be able to start a new life, but never heard from her again.

When we arrived home and received the literature from the Mennonites we liked their determination to live by the standards of the Bible; it was quite extremely different from what we had seen in other churches. Being convinced this was what God wanted for us, we up and moved to this town and attended the Mennonite church.

I was not allowed by my husband to take our son with us. But later as it turned out, Gabriel could not manage the school schedule and his work schedule; so he let me take Lew and I put him in school there. I lived a mile or two from a country school, so this arrangement worked well. I was so happy to have Lew with us again.

The teaching I received from the Mennonites compelled me to be reconciled to my husband. Their way is that of non-resistance. The wife is subject to the husband. So I yielded to whatever my husband decided to do. This was the beginning of the most horrifying years of my life.

Nevertheless, at a church service I prayed that God would give me an unconditional love for my husband, and that I could love him the way God loved him. This God did for me, and it was a love that I could hardly bare because of the circumstances. Gabriel by this time wanted nothing to do with me.

Although the first year I was allowed to have my son, the following five years I was not. I was only given visitation every other holiday and half of the summer. This first year Lew was in third grade. He was very young. He loved me very much and when we were separated it was damaging to him and to me. My husband took another woman into the home. His attitude toward me was very cold and distant. He did not regard me as a parent after that. I was never considered or consulted on any issue concerning our son. The separation took me near to death.

The Mennonites watched after my physical needs the three years that I lived there in their congregation. I opened a daycare in my home the first year, and barely squeaked by financially. Then I took a Certified Nurse Aide course, was licensed and began working in the nursing home.

My older son, Jim, was attending high school the first year we were there. He and Lew were still in constant conflict. Jim was malicious toward me, also. I wonder if all the conflict between the boys was really targeted toward me. Things became unbearable in the home. I did not realize at that time that Jim's behavior was largely the result of the unsettled life we lived during his formative years. Had I understood at that time, I would have done things so differently. I was desperate for mental respite. I sought counseling from ministers who never took interest. So I contacted a friend back in our home town and they took Jim into their home. They had a son the same age and our boys were friends. But things did not go well there so he asked my sister to take him in and she did.

As a younger child his behavior was more than I could bare at times and I sought respite from my family. He was devastated by this. He saw it as I did not love him. To him it was rejection. But to me it was only a time to rest and recuperate for a little season. My mental state was already ravaged by my former relationships. I had begun to suffer physically and still I did not recognize my condition, nor did I have any education in these maladies. I loved my son and do to this day, but my ability to endure was limited.

This left me alone for some years; I was working in the nursing home. I was so devastated at the breaking of our family I could hardly continue to breathe. I cried for hours every day. I worked the second shift at the nursing home. I remember being so sad and disoriented that when I came out of a patient's room I could not remember where I was. Often I could not hold back the tears so I would duck into a linen closet and cry. At night when I got home I would fall to my knees and pray for hours, begging God to save my husband and bring our family back together. My knees became calloused. This went on for months. I cried constantly. Really no one came to visit me. Besides going to church and having Sunday dinner somewhere I did not have much interaction with the Mennonites. I felt so alone with my grief. It was me and God. I know His heart was broken, too. He brought scriptures to me about what He was doing and would do: scriptures about healing. I had things to learn about giving it all to Him, about surrender and dying to self. I learned the hard way.

I came to a point when I could not go on, I was dying of sadness. At night I would have chest pains and really thought I was having a heart attack. I called a sister who was a nurse to ask for advice. She did not advise I call an ambulance. So I lived through many of these scary nights. I did see a cardiologist and he diagnosed me with an "electrical abnormality". My heart was leaping and skipping beats. Chest pains were shooting up my throat and down my left arm. But he said the drug to correct it was more dangerous than the condition. So I just lived with this condition and trusted God to keep me alive if He had use of me in this world.

I also developed severe dizzy spells during these years. They were short and positional. But just one spell was so devastating it was like a migraine headache, and left you as if you were recovering from one. They were sickening and I hated them, but lived with them for fourteen years before I figured out what was causing them. It was a milk allergy and I was a big milk drinker.

I begged God night and day to change this situation with my husband and He began to give me dreams and scriptures that told me of a coming calamity for my husband. I thought that in this devastation he would find God and in so doing our family would come back together. I realized that unless he did find God things would be the same as before. I lived in agony because of my love for my husband. I wanted salvation for him and for the life that only Jesus could provide for him and for our family.

> **Jeremiah 30:12-15** For thus saith the LORD, Thy bruise *is* incurable, *and* thy wound *is* grievous. *There is* none to plead thy cause, that thou mayest be bound up: thou hast no healing medicines. All thy lovers have forgotten thee; they seek thee not; for I have wounded thee with the wound of an enemy, with the chastisement of a cruel one, for the multitude of thine iniquity; *because* thy sins were increased. Why criest thou for thine affliction? thy sorrow *is* incurable for the multitude of thine iniquity: *because* thy sins were increased, I have done these things unto thee.

> **Job 33:14-30** For God speaketh once, yea twice, *yet man* perceiveth it not. In a dream, in a vision of the night, when deep sleep falleth upon men, in slumberings upon the bed; Then he openeth the ears of men,

> and sealeth their instruction, That he may withdraw man *from his* purpose, and hide pride from man. He keepeth back his soul from the pit, and his life from perishing by the sword. He is chastened also with pain upon his bed, and the multitude of his bones with strong *pain*: So that his life abhorreth bread, and his soul dainty meat. His flesh is consumed away, that it cannot be seen; and his bones *that* were not seen stick out. Yea, his soul draweth near unto the grave, and his life to the destroyers. If there be a messenger with him, an interpreter, one among a thousand, to shew unto man his uprightness: Then he is gracious unto him, and saith, Deliver him from going down to the pit: I have found a ransom. His flesh shall be fresher than a child's: he shall return to the days of his youth: He shall pray unto God, and he will be favourable unto him: and he shall see his face with joy: for he will render unto man his righteousness. He looketh upon men, and *if any* say, I have sinned, and perverted *that which was* right, and it profited me not; He will deliver his soul from going into the pit, and his life shall see the light. Lo, all these *things* worketh God oftentimes with man, To bring back his soul from the pit, to be enlightened with the light of the living.

In all this God wanted to communicate with me. He was getting through to me, and in ways that were beyond human. One night as I was sleeping, it actually was in the wee hours of the morning; I was lying on my back, and the Lord bumped my feet so that it rocked my whole body up toward my head. Immediately the morning song of a robin pierced the silence and I heard the Lord's voice. He said to me, "This is the morning of the resurrection of the dead; arise and pray, fore your husband is weeping". I arose and knelt beside my bed and prayed for Gabriel's lost soul. It was 4:00 AM. I did not understand the significance of this whole incident but in actuality I was praying for a time in the future that my husband would weep at 4:00 AM, it was the time of his resurrection from his dead soul, the resurrection in Christ Jesus. At the time, of course, I thought it was now and that my husband would become "born again" and we would all be together again.

18.

MY CROSS

Time went on and we shared our son over the holidays. We had a half way point where we met at a little restaurant that looked out over a big river. Many winter trips were made over the years. One woeful day I was returning my son to his dad, he was asleep in the back seat so I did not wake him when I went into a gas station for coffee. But I did lock the car doors. As I walked to the station I slipped on the ice. My feet went straight out in front of me and my weight came full force down on my seat. This was not the first time I had landed like this on my seat, fore it had happened several times in my past with serious complications. So this accident took its toll. I could not move. Someone came and helped me to get up and inside the building. I leaned over a bar stool and there I stayed, I was in excruciating pain. The attendant called an ambulance and they arrived in short order. I told them my little son was in the car. They went to get him but the doors were locked. They did not want to scare him but they had to wake him up. So they gently knocked on the door and got him to come inside. Together we rode in the ambulance to the hospital. We made a phone call to the restaurant where my husband was to meet us. When he arrived there, they told him the predicament. So Gabriel came to the hospital.

My mind was so desperate to be reunited with my husband, which is all I thought about. I was sure he would have compassion and take me in his arms, offer to bring me home and take care of me. I obviously was not going to be able to take care of myself. But, oh, what a woeful day it was. He did not take me into his arms and had no compassion on me. Rather he just took our son and left.

So as it turned out I called the Mennonites. A couple came, and got me and delivered me to a minister's home where they had offered to take care of me. They were dear to me and loved me so much. I needed their love for I was hurting more in my heart than in my seat.

I made an appointment with an orthopedic specialist and had an MRI done. I had knocked out a disc in my lower back. The doctor told me I would have to lie flat on my back until it went back in. This I did faithfully because it hurt so bad, I could do little else. So this older couple took me in for a month and waited on me hand and foot. I had dogs at home, so the neighbors fed them until I could return home. I so wanted to go home and be sad by myself with my dogs. As soon as I could stand long enough to cook my own meals, I went home. I was down on my back for most of six months.

This was a time of great depression and oppression. Circumstances had me in a prison of sorrow because I wanted it to be different so badly, I was hopelessly depressed. I prayed constantly and looked out the window from my couch at the tree tops and the sky. I cried seemingly unceasingly. I got few visits, but occasionally at first someone would bring me a casserole. One day as I lay on the couch bawling, a knock came to the door. As I answered it in tears, there stood two sisters who came to visit me. They were cousins or something; one of them was from Canada. She had a story to tell, as she had once an unfaithful husband. She was now divorced and single. She tried to encourage me to look to Jesus for my strength and go on. I could tell she had lived through much sorrow also. We could cry together. I do not remember if I was able to rise out of my grief but it was nice of them to go out of their way to comfort me.

Depression and oppression are cups full of hopelessness. They are overwhelming. A person finds themselves in despair; a prison that cannot be escaped. I became so engulfed that I was near death: real physical death. When our hearts are so broken how can they beat? And every sinew in my body was infiltrated with this sadness. I did not know then that my health was indeed being destroyed.

After six months of living in this state of sorrow I was able to at least start some kind of a job. My next door neighbor offered me a babysitting job for her four sons. The youngest was old enough to walk so I did not have to lift him. This was a God send; I took the job and started immediately. It was difficult to work and be happy for these lively boys, but I faked it and they never knew the difference.

One spring night as I knelt in prayer, I poured out my heart to Jesus. I told him that I was going to die of sadness if He did not change things. So He gave me a vision of His cross: it was lying on the ground empty. He told me I, too, had to die on that cross. I told Him I could lie down on it, but I could not nail in the spikes. He told me He would do it. So I lay down and spread out my arms and He nailed in the spikes. Then He raised me to the sky, which was dark and foreboding, and there I agonized unto death. This was a supernatural event because I had no power to put my old man to death, nor could I take away my sorrow. I certainly could not change my husband or reunite our family. I was powerless over life's oppressive circumstances. How could a mother actually be happy when her child is taken away from her and made to live under a roof where there was another woman posing as "mom" and sleeping with his dad? He was so young and impressionable. This circumstance caused me such agony, I cannot explain in words. There were seemingly no answers, and it all looked so hopeless. Life was seeping out the cracks of my brain. I felt I could not live. I begged God to change my husband. But nothing changed. He only grew more and more cruel and hardened to my position as a mother. In fact I was not even considered a mother or a human being. But when this old man died on that cross, the sadness was lifted, the thorn of agony that pierced my heart was removed; I felt a peace come over me like a cloud, starting at my head and slowly encompassing my whole body. I was set free from that oppressive sadness. It was nothing I did; only to be willing to lay down on that cross. The rest was Jesus. He did it, and it was supernatural. Life again pulsed through my veins.

19.

CANCER

That summer when Lew was with me for six weeks, he was called by the Saviour; he was eleven years old. He responded to the call and gave his life completely to Jesus. He was born again and, oh, what a happy boy he was. His smile was from ear to ear. He had been so burdened with his sins that when the Lord came into his heart they were gone; so completely gone that I think one could not be happier.

We discussed what it would be like for a Christian under the setting at home with dad, and my son so wanted to stay with me, to live and go to church. He had made a lot of good friends. The church had their own school which would have been very good for him under the circumstances. We must of asked Dad if he could stay because his reply came that he could if that was what he wanted. But something unusual happened; I think one night as Lew was praying. He kept hearing a voice telling him, "Go back to your father". We were so uncertain at the time about it that we asked the church leaders what they thought. They told us it was from God. So he went back to his dad and started the school year.

Over that summer since I had miraculously "died to self", I was much happier and the burden was lifted- extremely so. It came to me that because previously I could not let go of my husband to God that I had His hands tied in a sense. So when I got out of God's way, He was able to carry out His plan. Yes, He had a plan in all this; it is something to remember when all we can see is dark, looming clouds. Things began to happen in my husband's life that was not good, such as his truck breaking down. I think it needed an engine. There was other like incidents. Things were falling apart in his life.

At that time Gabriel had won his first horse-logging contract. He had a team of green draft horses, and this was really his first time to be the "teamster". He was a master at timber falling, but he rarely got to drive the horses when they worked on a horse-logging contract. Lew was on the unit with him some and gave me a little insight to how badly it turned out. I really don't remember if he even finished the contract as he became sick and was vomiting blood. I think the horses were a bit of a trial as it was their first logging experience. With my husband's health in rapid decline the overall experience was a disaster. God was at work.

He went to the doctor shortly thereafter and she told him he had an ulcer. I suppose she gave him something for that. Time went by and his condition only worsened. Finally he went to a different doctor. They found the cancer in his stomach and scheduled him for surgery. They removed two thirds of his stomach. It had spread to the aorta artery and lymph nodes. The doctor did the best he could, but did not get it all. I was not informed at all. Gabriel later told me that he knew I would rush over and it would not be a good scene at the hospital with a wife and a mistress. I found out, though, in a roundabout way. A sister in the Lord, Elsie, that lived in our home town and was, with her family, attending the Mennonite services; was driving down town one day and the Lord began to speak to her, directing her where to turn and where

Cancer

to park and what store to go into. She followed the Lord's prompting and found herself at the Co-op looking at the bulletin board which had posted an announcement for a benefit supper to raise money for Gabriel Decker's hospital bills. So she inquired inside and they told her he had cancer. She called the Mennonite ministers where I lived and told them to contact me with the news. They did and indeed it was devastating news. But once again I imagined it would be the thing that would reunite the family. I immediately prepared to make the trip to see my husband. I knew it would be awkward if his girlfriend was there but I proceeded anyway. I went to Elsie's house to stay. She was a comfort to my ravaged soul. I made contact up to my husband that I was there. The coast was clear, the girlfriend was gone and his mother was out from California to care for him. It was January and about three weeks since the surgery.

When I arrived I was not prepared to see Gabriel in the condition he was in. It was winter and a lot of snow was on the ground. He had a bed set up downstairs near the stove. He was hooked up to I.V.'s. His face was ghostly white and sunken. He had lost a lot of weight and looked like death. I wanted to talk to him alone but this was not possible, until he unhooked his I.V. and we walked outdoors. He was still smoking cigarettes so this was routine to take a walk. I had little time to talk so I got to the point. I told him I loved him, and I wanted our family back together again. I wanted to come home and take care of him. He would have no part of it. So we returned to the house and waited for Lew to get home from school. I stayed till nearly dark, then Lew and I left for Elsie's house where we were together for a few days. When I left Dad's I could do nothing but cry. I remember on the little dirt road to Elsie's house I had to stop a few times to throw up because I was so sick with grief and bawling. My son did not know how to comfort me. I could hardly sleep that night; Elsie got up because she heard me crying, and prayed with me. She was such a comfort to me. I stayed the weekend and then my son had to go home so he could go back to school. I left for my home. I could not find a place of rest in my soul.

Gabriel's cancer had started in the stomach. The doctor told him it was because he ate so much lunch meat with nitrates. But he also chewed tobacco and you know a person has to swallow a lot of the juice. He had been working hard for a few years and as I described it, "he was burning the candle at both ends". Before we separated he was on a logging unit that was about two and a half hours away. There were a few fellows in the neighborhood who worked the unit also. Gabriel would pick them all up in the wee hours of the morning. He was always the driver because he had the truck. So while the fellows all slept, he drank coffee. They worked for seven hours then drove home. So they were on the road for five hours a day on top of their working hours. I could see my husband getting sick then. You could see it in his face, I was worried about him. I appealed to his boss to rent a cabin near the unit so they did not have to commute every day. This he did, and that took a lot of pressure off Gabriel. Then he only came home on the weekends.

After surgery Gabriel opted to forgo chemo and approached the cancer with a special diet. Some months later he had a good report and let down his guard. He chose to go back to college to learn a desk job. This added to his stress load. He attended college for two years and did receive his associate's degree.

Time went on and Gabriel contacted me and asked me to sign off on the deed to our land and home. This was so devastating to me, it just looked like doom. I was so upset, imagining him living there with this woman on the land that he and I had worked so hard to develop into a home. They together were living there with my son as theirs and not mine. I was sick with despair. As I prayed to the Father He spoke to me and said, "Trust Me." I said, "Okay Lord I will trust you and comply".

But I asked Him to stop the flood waters of my tears, and to inhibit the tentacles of sorrow that branched from my heart into all of my body. This He granted and still to this day it is so. It was like He built a dam to hold back my tears. I could only cry for a few minutes and then I could not cry any more. And the sorrow was contained inside my heart. My body was not permeated. This was a mile marker in my life because what He does is forever and even today my crying is limited and the sorrow is shallow waters. Sometimes I wonder if I am without feelings.

Gabriel's symptoms returned and he went to the doctor for another scan. They did not take the picture of the right areas and missed the cancer. Time went on and he returned to the doctor and this time they found the cancer to be quite advanced.

20.

DID HE REPENT?

The Mennonite church had previously started a mission in our home town near my husband's new place. He had sold the farm and put a down on a house in town. This is when I decided to move back to the county. When I arrived I found out from my son that Gabriel's girl friend had moved out. I knew it was all in the Lord's timing as I do not know if I could have bore the grief of that relationship. So then with me in the same town as my husband I was able to see my son every other weekend. He could get on and off the school bus just outside our door. This was a great relief. But my husband did not want to see me. As he got sicker his mother returned to take care of him. I was not welcome to come to the house. A few times, though, the Lord prompted me to prepare a gift and go now to see my husband. I was able in this way to be blessed to see him two weeks before he died.

I started a new job the day he passed. That night my son had stayed the night with me and I was going to drop him at his dad's on my way to work. His mother called me early and asked me to come a few minutes before scheduled as she had something to share with me, so I did, Lew went into his bedroom and I stayed in the car. The door to

Did he Repent?

Lew's dad's room was closed so Lew did not know what had happened. My mother-in-law came, sat in the car and told me my husband had passed away at about 4:00 AM. I was shocked and devastated because so far I was not aware that he had repented of his sins and had never apologized to me about the adultery. I had believed God would save his soul. I was pierced to the core of my heart. I went straight into my son's room and told him. We both wailed; we thought Dad would repent and we would all be back together again. I felt sure God would heal his cancer if only he would have given his heart to Him. But there was no evidence of any repentance.

After reporting to my employer, my son and I went to the funeral home to view Dad's (my husband) body. He was not ready for viewing but we still wanted to see him. I could not believe he was really gone. When we saw him his body was still warm, I begged God to bring him back. We wailed. Both of us got down on our knees and prayed, please God don't let him go to hell; bring him back. Finally with tears streaming down our faces we kissed him good bye forever and left.

We went back to my husband's house, got Lew's clothes and things, then left without any hesitation. From that day forward my son and I were a family again; at least 'till he grew up. He was fourteen.

My older son had joined the Navy and he was notified of his dad's death. He immediately boarded a plane and came home for two weeks. We had a memorial service at the Mennonite church. Then my mother-in-law planned one, too, at her church, and the burial followed. He was buried in an old country graveyard in the tiny mountain town where we lived for about twelve years. We were not informed of the service that Granma had planned until the boys showed up at their dad's house the evening before to visit, as Granpa had flown in. Then they said, "Oh, there is a funeral service tomorrow, if you want to come; and your mom". Of course we wanted to go! This was my husband and the boy's dad. The funeral service was very formal and after there was refreshments. We stood in a line to shake hands with those who came. My husband's mistress was there and she shook everyone's hand but avoided me. But she was now part of the family because she married my husband's brother. I was treated like I was not family. This was very grievous to me.

We went on to the graveyard; which may have been a separate day. There were some testimonies spoken. I read some scriptures about love.

> **Song of Solomon 8:6-7** Set me as a seal upon thine heart, as a seal upon thine arm: for love *is* strong as death; jealousy *is* cruel as the grave: the coals thereof *are* coals of fire, *which hath* a most vehement flame. Many waters cannot quench love, neither can the floods drown it: if a man would give all the substance of his house for love, it would utterly be contemned.

There were some funny things spoken about Gabriel always being late. I told a story of how he use to carry Jimmy up the mountain late in the night when he was asleep. But it all seemed so humiliating as I was the outcast. My husband's former mistress, then married to his brother, threw a white rose on the casket as she stood right beside me. Elsie, my dear sister, sang Amazing Grace. It was so beautiful. Then the men that were there started throwing shovelfuls of dirt on the casket, I totally lost my composure and bawled. My friends lead me away. It was finished.

I inherited all belongings which were things we had accumulated over the eleven years we were together, along with vehicles, bank accounts and the house. My mother-in-law stayed about two weeks, then left for her home. My older son returned to the Navy and my younger son and I moved into the house my husband left us. It was a double-wide that was well-kept. It had an addition on one side and a root cellar. This was the nicest house I had ever lived in since leaving my parents'. We were so thankful. But there was unrest because Dad, my husband was gone, and where in eternity was he? I spoke with my old minister friend back where I joined the Mennonites over the phone. He gave me courage that we don't know if my husband repented at the last hour, like the thief on the cross that hung next to Jesus. I was so caught in the whirlwind that I did not remember when God woke me up in the wee hours of the morning many months previous, saying to me, "This is the morning of the resurrection of the dead, arise and pray fore your husband is weeping". It was at 4:00 AM and my husband died at 4:00 AM. At that time when God awoke me from my sleep, I was praying for my husband during his final hour of life.

Then nine months later I had a dream I know was from God. I think He waits till the whirlwind of our mind comes to a calm, then He speaks so we can hear Him. This was the dream:

I was hiding in some bushes; the sky was dark and looming with heavy black clouds. I was in a court-yard of a castle where my husband was a prisoner. They had hung him from a cross with ropes. I could see him from my hiding place: he was writhing in pain, mumbling and moaning. He was near death. I was looking for my chance to set him free, but there were guards pacing back and forth. Finally my chance came; they were out of sight. I ran for the cross, shimmied up and cut the ropes that held my husband's hands and feet. As I did, he fell in a crumple to the ground. But as soon as he fell, he pounced to his feet and ran away into the castle. I followed him and found some people standing around looking at a map of the castle. It had been placed there by some carpenters who worked on the construction of the castle; my husband was one of them. I knew he knew the way through the castle with its many passages and rooms. I began to follow a passage that led down to a floor below. It was a ramp rather than stairs. I looked out a window and saw some children playing. I went out to them and asked them if they had seen my husband. They said, "No", so I returned to the castle and was following that passageway when I passed a butler pushing a cart of food. I asked him if he had seen my husband and he conveyed secretly that he was in the kitchen. So I proceeded down the corridor to the kitchen and I stood a distant away because I did not want to give away my husband's cover. I stood in a room that was open to the kitchen and I saw him working with the other chefs. My husband was dressed in pure white, including a chef's hat. He saw me and flashed a quick smile. I took it as a gesture of thanks. Guards soon appeared and were asking if anyone had seen their prisoner. No one gave him away and soon they continued their search. My eyes caught my husband's and at the same time we walked out back doors into the wide open spaces. Beyond us was the ocean. We could not walk together nor speak to each other. But we both walked to the edge of the ocean water. My husband crossed the land water barrier and continued to walk out and he did not look back. I knew that he was entering eternity and I could not go, it was not my time.

I awoke from my dream and I knew it was from the Lord. He was telling me that my husband prayed and found salvation. The pure white garments were the righteousness of the saints which only comes from Jesus' blood. The little smile was his thanks to me for my prayers which are what cut him down from his cross. The guards were Satan's angels who kept my husband imprisoned. I knew without a doubt that he found salvation, but it was only at the last hour before death and no man witnessed it. It was only he and God, and then he crossed over the great divide.

I began to understand that the healing I thought I would see was spiritual instead of physical. The Lord knew what was right to do in our family. This had to be this way for the good of us all. Maybe my husband would have never been able to walk as a Christian so in God's mercy He took him as soon as he was 'born again'. It took me a long time to sort it all out, and for the pain of my wounds to heal enough that I could see the overall picture.

21.

HEPATITIS

The scriptures that had flooded my devotions about healing continued to flow. Within the next year I realized that I was the one He would heal physically. Unbeknownst to me I had contracted Hepatitis C virus (HCV) back when I was a teenager after my boyfriend Jim put a needle in my arm. It takes about 25 years to destroy 90% of the liver. Only when you are down to the remaining 10% of the liver do functions begin to fail. I was experiencing extreme fatigue and inability to digest foods. One day at work there was a magazine on the desk about HCV, and I read it. I had the symptoms. Some time previous, I had received word that my former boyfriend Jim, the father of my first son, had this disease and was dying. I was pretty sure I could have contracted it from him, when he used his needle to hit me up with the heroin. So I went for tests. The tests that were run were not conclusive for the diagnosis and the doctor told me I did not have HCV. So I went on my way but only became sicker and sicker. I studied and learned that the tests the doctor ran were of no value for diagnosis. I went back and ordered the proper test. When the results came in they informed me that I did indeed have HCV.

So I began to alter my diet, find the foods that I could digest and I tried hard to hold my job, but I was so fatigued it was difficult.

We were living in this house in town that I inherited from my husband; my oldest son was now living at home as he was no longer in the Navy. Some of their old friends came around and got the boys to go to parties. I did not appreciate this as my youngest was a Christian. This was all instrumental in watering down his faith and obedience to God. It became so threatening that it was not really a profitable thing to remain living in this town. So I put the house up for sale and looked for a place in the country. After much searching and praying I found the "land of my inheritance", as the Lord portrayed to me. **Joshua 14:9** And Moses sware on that day, saying, Surely the land whereon thy feet have trodden shall be thine inheritance, and thy children's for ever, because thou hast wholly followed the LORD my God.

The land had no structures, but there was a creek and a lot of deciduous trees. I liked this as it reminded me of where I grew up. The Lord confirmed to me through the scriptures that this was to be my home.

It did not sit well with some of the Mennonites and there was a lot of resistance, even dissension. I think, because they thought a woman should not attempt building up a place and are better suited to be in some little house on a street in town. But one old minister came to visit our congregation because there were no ministers here. He listened to my story and liked it. He said to me, "It looks like an open door". So I proceeded and closed the deal, but the sparks were flying because I was doing this. There was a lot of persecution and oppression in the works. I did not yield to their attempts to control my life. Rather, I was listening to God and following Him, resulting in a lot of stress for me. The issue had to be brought up in a revival and when I brought in the facts before the ministers, the deacon that had been assigned as overseer of this new congregation, the one who caused such a stirring of the bees' nest in my land purchase; became sorry for his action and apologized. So we went on, but the issue never died in many of their hearts and some years later they still used it as a spear to wound and accuse me. It took me much time and suffering to get beyond this thing. It was my second experience of their assertion of control and manipulation. Which I knew was not of God at the time but I did not catch on that their whole system was to blame.

> **Proverbs 14:1** Every wise woman buildeth her house: but the foolish plucketh it down with her hands.

The first offense had been when this same deacon demanded that I sell my horse Fairy Dancer, which I had raised from a filly. She was like a member of our family and a very intimate part of me. I was poor at the time and he thought I should not have this animal. I was forced into a corner. Since we were expected to do whatever a staff member mandated, or we were be put on church work, which means that your case is brought to the staff; I opted to "give" the horse to a friend with children for the time bein'. I did this and she was with them for a few years until I was in a place where I could have her and had the income to take care of her. This forcefulness was very offensive to me and something that did not feel as it had come from my beloved Lord. But I still was not enlightened … not yet.

22.
THE HEALING PRAYER

To get closer to where my new land was, and to get out of town; I moved into a shop on one of the Mennonite's property. They were a local family that did not grow up with this faith and did things more the way I would have as far as living rurally and growing a garden and healing our diseases with herbs. Any way we set this shop up very nice and had an outhouse nearby. It was just my younger son and I. My older son moved to the city to work and get into college. We rented out the house in town while it was listed for sale. I was still holding my job, though my health was getting worse and worse.

The church sister on who's yard we lived was very gracious to help me all she could to maintain my life. She grew wheat grass and juiced it with carrots for me every day. This gave me healing power and nutrition as my diet was becoming very narrow. My friends were becoming quite concerned for me. I had lost weight from about one hundred eighteen to ninety nine pounds. My face was ashen grey. My strength was waning constantly. It took about eight to twelve hours to digest a meal. So food sat in my stomach and soured. I was nauseated a lot. I had all the symptoms of HCV. My blood platelets were low and I easily bled. I had brain fog and confusion. In spite of it all I held my job, my boss understood.

During revivals I asked for a "healing prayer". This was given to me and was an experience I will never forget. I believed God would heal me as the scriptures about healing had been coming to me for a long time already.

> **John 11:4** When Jesus heard *that*, he said, This sickness is not unto death, but for the glory of God, that the Son of God might be glorified thereby.

> **Matthew 9:22** But Jesus turned him about, and when he saw her, he said, Daughter, be of good comfort; thy faith hath made thee whole. And the woman was made whole from that hour.

> **James 5:14-16** Is any sick among you? let him call for the elders of the church; and let them pray over him, anointing him with oil in the name of the Lord: And the prayer of faith shall save the sick, and the Lord shall raise him up; and if he have committed sins, they shall be forgiven him. Confess *your* faults one to another, and pray one for another, that ye may be healed. The effectual fervent prayer of a righteous man availeth much.

I explained this to the visiting ministers and they felt it was of God. As I knelt down with Lew beside me, the older minister anointed me with oil and laid his hands on my shoulders. I felt the healing power of God come through his hands. It was a warmth that started at my shoulders and went down through my whole body. I knew I was healed. The next morning I sat up in bed, took my Bible and the scriptures came to me as such:

Luke 8:48 And he said unto her, Daughter, be of good comfort: thy faith hath made thee whole; go in peace.

Luke 8:55 And her spirit came again, and she arose straightway: and he commanded to give her meat.

Luke 13:12 And when Jesus saw her, he called *her to him*, and said unto her, Woman, thou art loosed from thine infirmity.

There were other scriptures that were about being healed. I just knew I was well and that I would no longer need the herbs to help me digest my foods and heal my liver.

That day I was invited to Elsie's for lunch. This is the story she tells, not knowing whether I was healed or not. Previously I had been unable to digest proteins and fats. She prayed to the Lord, "What am I going to make for her that she can eat?" She heard the Lord tell her, "Serve her venison". And indeed she did. I ate it and digested it in the proper time and did not become nauseated. We both rejoiced and praised God for the healing. So as the days progressed I was strong and felt young again, I think God just gave me a new liver.

When summer came I began construction on my new place, step by step. After I built the outhouse, I constructed the barn, which I wanted to live in while I constructed the rest of the buildings and dug the well. But to live in the barn, I was discouraged by the church men, so I gave it up. I had to purchase a strip of land to get in a road, not knowing whether a bull dozer would hit solid rock and we could not get it in. We had to cut into a hill and go over the top of it. But the Lord gave me scriptures that assured me He would make a road for me.

Isaiah 40:4 Every valley shall be exalted, and every mountain and hill shall be made low: and the crooked shall be made straight, and the rough places plain:

1 Samuel 27:10 And Achish said, Whither have ye made a road to day? And David said, Against the south of Judah, and against the south of the Jerahmeelites, and against the south of the Kenites.

This road was to be cut in on the south border of the neighboring property. This scripture described the situation so well I marveled. I had an easement through that property but the land owner put up a fight to keep me from using it. This man is one that did not get along with people very well and was not at all attempting to be peaceable. His renters were instructed to stop me from using the easement road. I had already built my barn and was storing my belongings there. So I needed to get in and out. My real estate agent was not happy with the situation. A gate was constructed across the easement and so I opted to hike in from there on the ranch to the south of the forbidden property, which I had permission to do. On occasion I ran into the owner of the forbidden property and received a verbal assault. I am not accustomed to such language and I really wanted nothing to do with this man. Finally he put up a gate and a lock across the first easement road which was not the easement in question. Other property owners had the right to use this road. So when I found this to be the case I reported to my real estate agent and he went out to have a word or two with this man, who actually lived several hours away, but was there to cause me trouble. He was residing at his rental house with the tenants. Now my real estate agent is not a man you want to fool around with, and as he left to go up there he notified the sheriff to let him know that he was going up to confront this man and if he wished to be involved he needed to start out in that direction. And indeed he did and arrived with us. This put the forbidden property owner in a quandary. He was required by the sheriff to remove the lock and stop this foolishness.

Finally I had to report the goings on to the investors from whom I purchased my property. They were upset about this and filed a law suit. But before the case could be finalized I had to sign my name to the documents to sue this man. I just could not do this because of the scriptures that teach us to not fight our enemies but rather give them even more than they ask for. **Matthew 5:44** But I say unto you, Love your enemies, bless them that curse you, do good to them that hate you, and pray for them which despitefully use you, and persecute you;

> **Matthew 5:40** And if any man will sue thee at the law, and take away thy coat, let him have *thy* cloke also.

> **Romans 12:20** Therefore if thine enemy hunger, feed him; if he thirst, give him drink: for in so doing thou shalt heap coals of fire on his head.

So the men who sold me the property gave me an option of discounting me on the sale price if I excused them of their responsibility to provide access to my property. I agreed. So I inquired to the land owner on the south border of the contested easement road if they might sell me a strip of land just wide enough to put in a road. So with confidence from the Lord in the scriptures mentioned I purchased a strip of land and trusted God to get in a road. The bulldozer driver was a Christian also and he marveled at these scriptures. It went like God had said and it was a goodly road.

Next came the well: it was just a shallow well and bein's I was close to the creek the water came in at about four feet. It was a good well and I was very happy.

Then with only $5000.00 and a lot of faith I started the daylight basement of the house. I was able to hire carpenters and pour the concrete. Then Elsie and her husband offered to give me a loan and so the construction took off. I paid them with the rent money from the house in town. When it was all done to the point that we had something to take shelter under, we moved in. It was December and winter was blowing and spittin' at our walls. We had insulation in the downstairs which was to be the main part of the house. The upstairs had nothing; not even interior walls. The downstairs had a temporary kitchen sink, a toilet and a bathtub. The refrigerator and range were plugged in. We could live well and we did. We were so happy to have our own house, and of course we were warm because we had a big wood stove. I wanted real brick chimneys, so there was one for the heat stove and one for the cook stove in the kitchen. This was all made possible with a lot of helping hands from the boys from the church, my son and me. The carpenters took the time to teach us things and to put us to good work. It was an awesome feeling to have a good roof over our heads and warmth wrapped around us as old man winter blew at our door.

From that point forward the continuation of the construction came in small increments. I used my minimum wage to buy as many materials as possible. My son, I and a family of sheet rockers did the work. My mother gave us inheritance money after daddy died, a little at a time, which helped. It took years to complete the house, but it came together and has been a blessing from God that I would have never imagined. And the beauty around me is like a drink of cold water on a hot day. I drink it in constantly and oh, how gracious is my Lord as He knew I would need this place to soothe my broken spirit, body and soul.

23.
GOING DOWN TO THE DUNGHILL

As time moved forward the church in this community grew with the addition of families from other areas. They are encouraged to establish new congregations. An elderly minister and wife moved in and a new church building was built, along with the school as Mennonites have their own schools.

Life in the church became hard, especially for us ones coming from the outside, as we did not quite fit the bill. My friend Elsie, her children and husband were all expelled. They wanted out after so much abuse. They were smarter than I. They caught on sooner that these people operate after the doctrines of men rather than God. She and her family were just not perfect enough, and their children were always in trouble at school, which then brought the discipline on to the parents. They were constantly on the "hot seat", as we called it. Finally they just stopped going to church and pretty much put their foot down. They would not allow the ministers to accuse them anymore. When they were expelled we all had to hold the avoidance, or shunning; on them. This was grievous to me, but because of this I drifted away from my dear, beloved friend. It really was a great loss.

Life and death unfolded here. Another minister and his wife came to live. This was a more permanent situation. They started a successful business and built a new home. This minister pulled a lot of weight in the church. He was from the old school. We locals were of quite a different sort. I, being a former hippie and a hillbilly from way back, ate beets and turnips and other weird food. I was always teased. But really I think there was more to it than just fun.

When revivals would come around I often mentioned my need of counseling about the past and the effects of it that I still suffered mentally, spiritually and physically. But my request always fell on deaf ears. I always thought that a real godly church was about lifting out a compassionate hand to the suffering. I often asked if the ministers would pray a healing prayer and anoint me with oil. I never would get back an answer; they just ignored me. It took me a while to catch on what this was all about. This church was all about the outward appearance of righteousness and not the heart and soul of men. I was a heart and soul sort of person and I was not interested so much in this outward appearance. Jesus sent out His apostles to heal the sick, this just made no sense to me. But the Lord was giving me scriptures and they certainly applied to these ministers.

> **Luke 9:1-2** Then he called his twelve disciples together, and gave them power and authority over all devils, and to cure diseases. And he sent them to preach the kingdom of God, and to heal the sick.

> **Ezekiel 34:4** The diseased have ye not strengthened, neither have ye healed that which was sick, neither have ye bound up *that which was broken*, neither have ye brought again that which was driven away, neither have ye sought that which was lost; but with force and with cruelty have ye ruled them.

The separation of my family and the death of my husband took a huge toll on my health and my brain. Insomnia was plaguing my nights and I was suffering continuous dizzy spells, they were quite severe. God saw fit to help me and by His hand I got rid of the dizzy spells through the process of elimination of dairy products. But still I did not catch on totally what was the source of my problem. One night I was down on my knees after these spells had overtaken me again, I prayed, "Father what is causing these dizzy spells?" and I heard Him say, "It's the milk". Wow! I got it. I had been off of it for a while and they had stopped. When I started back on it again, they came back. Well, I could work with this. I got off the milk and the dizzy spells left me-finally!

Oh, but little did I know what kind of persecution I would suffer for not "blending" in with the "in crowd". I had to cut out cheese and butter and all that good stuff. So at other people's houses and at potlucks I always had to ask, "What's in that and did you make your bread with milk...?" So by the end of the serving line I was able to eat very little, but I was not grieved because it was a little price to pay for being dizzy-free. The minister looking on was grieved because I set myself apart and did not blend. So the persecution began, mostly behind my back as I was declared "self diagnosed". So I was walking a fine line. Being a highly-sensitive person I caught on to all the accusations and feared I would be expelled. When you are taken in by the indoctrination of this group, one believes, like they all do, that to be expelled is an automatic death sentence in hell. So I lived in a constant underlying fear. This wreaks havoc on the health and brain. I was on a downhill spiral that gained momentum rapidly.

Isaiah 9:16 For the leaders of this people cause *them* to err; and *they that are* led of them *are* destroyed.

Ezekiel 22:7 In thee have they set light by father and mother: in the midst of thee have they dealt by oppression with the stranger: in thee have they vexed the fatherless and the widow.

Exodus 22:22-24 Ye shall not afflict any widow, or fatherless child. If thou afflict them in any wise, and they cry at all unto me, I will surely hear their cry; And my wrath shall wax hot, and I will kill you with the sword; and your wives shall be widows, and your children fatherless.

Zechariah 7:9-13 Thus speaketh the LORD of hosts, saying, Execute true judgment, and shew mercy and compassions every man to his brother: And oppress not the widow, nor the fatherless, the stranger, nor the poor; and let none of you imagine evil against his brother in your heart. But they refused to hearken, and pulled away the shoulder, and stopped their ears, that they should not hear. Yea, they made their hearts *as* an adamant stone, lest they should hear the law, and the words which the LORD of hosts hath sent in his spirit by the former prophets: therefore came a great wrath from the LORD of hosts. Therefore it is come to pass, *that* as he cried, and they would not hear; so they cried, and I would not hear, saith the LORD of hosts:

Job 41:24 His heart is as firm as a stone; yea, as hard as a piece of the nether *millstone*.

I always had to hold a job, but my ability to work full-time waned. Soon I fell out with Meniere's Disease. This is devastating dizzy spells that are a result of a rupture in the inner ear. It occurs when there is an electrolyte imbalance. Electrolytes are regulated by the adrenal glands. These spells would last about eight hours. I was under the care of an ear, nose and throat specialist in a city a few hours' drive from home. On my second visit, the deacon, with his wife, was assigned the task of driving me to my appointment. I had told the two ministers and the deacon the night before that the doctor had told me, "I am sorry to tell you but there are no drugs to stop these attacks". The minister, apparently, did not believe me. So secretly he assigned the deacon the task of going into the examination room with the doctor to find out, the best I could figure, if I was refusing to take the drugs prescribed. This deacon was instructed to drive the speed limit since I voiced my fear of riding with him because of his driving record. I asked the minister to drive me but he declined. In my estimation, he did not want to be the one to go into the examination room to find out from the doctor if I was taking the prescribed drugs. When we arrived at the clinic the deacon informed me he wanted to come in the exam room with me. This took me by surprise and I said I would ask the doctor. She allowed it at a certain point. After they came in, she explained my condition to me, and never mentioned once the need for a drug. The deacon tried to interrupt her, but she overrode him and never allowed him to speak. I believe she perceived the same as I, that they were up to something fishy. So he never succeeded in his mission and I think he was mad. On the trip home he laid into me, accused me of not respecting doctors, and everything he could come up with to accuse me of. This was supposed to be a non-stressful trip. I had just had an attack two days before that left my body and brain traumatized to the point that my speech was slowed down and halted, and my vocabulary was mixed up. Stress only pushes me over the edge. Finally I had, had enough of his insults, I can't remember what I said but it was only one sentence. It shut him up right quick and for the rest of the trip.

This was the beginning of a life-threatening adrenal collapse. From then on I was not able to hold a job. I tried, but failed, and have been disabled ever since. With the help of my biological sister I found an herbal remedy called T-Bio that stopped the Meniere's attacks for which I am so thankful. To endure the spinning for eight hours is the most horrifying experience a person can imagine.

The doctor I was seeing referred me on to an E.N.T. neurosurgeon in another city. This time I arranged for my own transportation through the state. But when the deacon heard of it, he assigned a church woman to go with me. When she called, I told her I had already made arrangements for a ride. But she insisted in riding along. When we arrived, she told me she wanted to come into the exam room so she could learn about the disease. I was not happy about this, but allowed it. By this appointment date I had already found the vitamin herbal remedy that stopped the attacks. I took the informational flyer on the product T-Bio in to the doctor and asked him what it was in this formula that had stopped the attacks. He looked it over and said it was the bioflavonoids. Bioflavonoids directly support the adrenals and the regulation of aldosterone, the hormone that regulates the electrolytes. He told me to keep doing what I was doing, but if the spells came back to come see him again and he would prescribe a diuretic. I wonder if the church woman reported that a neurosurgeon prescribed that I stay on my vitamins and herbs to the deacon.

> **Isaiah 29:15** Woe unto them that seek deep to hide their counsel from the LORD, and their works are in the dark, and they say, Who seeth us? and who knoweth us?

I learned a lot about Meniere's Disease after I started studying the adrenals. The adrenals produce a hormone called aldosterone which controls the electrolytes. In the inner ear are two canals with concentrated fluids of sodium and potassium, which are electrolytes. The dizzy attacks happen when a canal bursts; the fluid damages the hearing and balance mechanisms: the signal the ear puts out to tell the brain the body position is stopped. The other ear gives the brain a signal one is spinning because there is no balanced signal between the two ears. This is my own interpretation gathered from information from books and doctors. I suggest doing your own research and gather your own explanation. Meniere's is nothing anyone wants to continue to endure, so try to keep your stress level down. Stress affects the adrenals that govern the electrolytes. Sleep is vital to the production of cortisol, your stress hormone produced by the adrenals. You have to get the deep alpha sleep and stay in it for several hours each night; when you are under stress; sometimes this just does not happen.

For those who do not understand the function of the adrenals I will give you a few basic facts. The adrenals are two small glands about the size of a walnut, situated on top of each kidney. They work with the kidneys and yet are very specific in function. They produce your hormones which govern a wide spectrum of body function. They are the primary generator, of sex hormones for women after menopause.

The adrenals are glands operating in the endocrine system. They work in sync with the hypothalamus in the brain and the pituitary gland in an axis, and work in harmony with the other glands of the endocrine system.

The adrenals equip the whole body's response to stress. Stress is not all bad; your body has to respond to any exhilarating event, whether it is joyous or traumatizing. The adrenals are the command station for many functions and are involved in immune response; therefore they play a role in auto-immune disease. When there are foreign invaders such as viruses, chemical drugs, or environmental chemicals that have invaded the body, the adrenals alert all systems to address the invaders. When the adrenals are over-worked and fail to do their assigned tasks, the whole body suffers and the immune system goes haywire. Failure to respond to these invaders can result in death. When your adrenals become more or less non-functional, your life is on the line. To continue to expose yourself to stress of any kind could cost you your life.

    I did not keep my stress level down and my condition worsened. I became so fatigued that normal routine was not possible. I could not walk far or exert in everyday activities. I have always used vitamins and herbs to treat my health and my children's, when they were growing up. I was doing all I could to build up the adrenal gland with my limited recourses. The persecution for taking vitamins and herbs as well as being on a special diet continued. It was a vicious cycle. I collapsed several times with adrenal failure in response to a stressor or stressful event. This includes a lack of response to a chemical drug. I was under the care of a local naturopath who diagnosed me with a severe case of adrenal insufficiency and put me on low dose hydrocortisone (cortisol). This was not enough to support life. My adrenals were failing. I was in the E.R. and hospitalized on several occasions. Most medical doctors do not know what they are dealing with as they are not trained to diagnosis and treat subclinical cases of Addison's Disease or adrenal insufficiency. The condition is called Hypoadrenocorticism. Some doctors just watched my vitals for seven hours 'till I could move my limbs again and then dismissed me from the E.R. Others, because of my medical alert necklace, actually saved my life with hydrocortisone IV's and saline drip. Some doctors were in total ignorance and nearly killed me.

    The symptoms in a collapse that make this condition life-threatening are low blood pressure and blood volume, poor circulation, low blood sugar, and low body temperature. One loses completely all muscle strength and mobility of your extremities, also affecting the heart muscle; resulting in collapse. Without immediate treatment with hydrocortisone a person can become comatose. Death can be the result. This happened to me at the dentist. I was non-responsive after an injection, transported by ambulance to the E.R. and the attending doctor did nothing to treat me. My son was notified, as his name and phone number were recorded as my emergency contact on the files at the dentist office. He was by my side within minutes. We waited it out for about six hours until I could be transported home. At that time I did not understand the condition completely but I did know it was adrenal failure. I did not have a doctor that knew how to diagnose or treat Hypoadrenocorticism. It was after this incident that I went to a Naturopathic doctor. Until then I was not yet on hydrocortisone.

On another occasion, sometime later and after being diagnosed by a naturopathic doctor and on low dose hydrocortisone, I spent one day in the E.R. and three days in the hospital. I nearly died in this occasion. I had collapsed at church during the women's Sunday school class. The conversation was stressful to me. I grew very weak and could not sit up. I dropped my Bible on the floor. The woman next to me helped me into the nursery where I collapsed on the floor. People gathered around me. Amongst them were two E.M.T.'s. The minister announced, thinking that I could not hear him, "It's a spirit". Soon I could not move and they called for an ambulance. They never even asked a prayer in my behalf.

The E.R. doctor treated me correctly with I.V. hydrocortisone and saline drip, because he read my medical alert necklace that stated I was sub-Addison's, and on hydrocortisone. He saved my life. After about six hours I was coming around and allowed to leave the E.R. with a family who offered to care for me. My son was by my side and stayed with me. As soon as the hydrocortisone I.V. wore off, I collapsed again and was transported back to the E.R. My body was like a rag doll and my blood pressure was so low the doctor was in denial. The minister from church came to the E.R. and talked with the doctor, conveying to him that I had been depressed since my mother died. I really wasn't depressed, but only suffering from the abuse of these leaders of the church. He also conveyed to the doctor that I was taking massive doses of magnesium sulfate. Evidently a woman in the church had told the minister that I was taking these doses of magnesium sulfate (Epsom salt) and the affects of doing so were the same as I was experiencing. Even though this was false information, many of them concluded it was my vitamins that were causing my breakdown.

    I will explain, magnesium sulfate is Epsom salt and it is used to soak your body in, such as a foot soak or in a bath. It works wonders for achey muscles or tendons. It is safely used for a laxative as directed on the package. But long-term use is not recommended. I use it only as directed upon occasion. I do take magnesium taurate by Cardiovascular Research, which in my opinion is the most assumable form of magnesium. This means your body uses it and very little is lost in the drought. You find the dose that is right for you by keeping it just under what would cause diarrhea. I take the recommended therapeutic dose of magnesium taurate to alleviate Fibromyalgia. Since I found this treatment I have little to no pain with Fibromyalgia. It also assists in sleep, which is vital for those suffering from adrenal failure as well as Fibromyalgia. My rheumatologist told me he would not put me on narcotics and told me to continue taking magnesium taurate.

    I was hospitalized for a few days. The E.R. doctor ordered my magnesium level to be tested and it came back perfectly normal. The doctor who took over my case while I was hospitalized, looked up all the vitamins and herbs that I was taking and told me when I was dismissed, to continue all of them. But I assume the church people excused themselves from all responsibility to me by concluding that all my problems were self-inflicted because I take vitamins and not drugs. Even though the minister's wives assured me that they would help me with my hospital bills not one penny was offered.

The doctor who took charge in the hospital was in denial of my diagnosis and his lack of treatment nearly took my life.

After being dismissed, I was opting to go to the clinic that specializes in adrenal disease, but the church held a "men's meeting" which was their custom in my affairs to control me and hold authority over me, under the guise of seeking God's will for my life. They decided they would not help me go there or support me in doing so, as there were naturopathic doctors in this clinic. One man told me I would "lose out" if I went there and he would not do my chores while I was gone. This "losing out" means the same as going to hell, so in spite of the fact I had just nearly expired at the hands of allopathic doctors, I yielded to their stupidity.

24.

THE LAST REVIVAL

A few months later a revival took place where the visiting ministers were prompted to take up the fight against those of us who use natural doctors and counselors, and take vitamins and herbs. So they came to my house to address the fact that I take "vitamins and herbs", and that I was "self-diagnosed", and that I had "books" in my house. This is kinda like accusing me of witchcraft. I told them that I did indeed take herbs and had books in my house and then I listed all the specialists I had been to that have diagnosed me with a long list of maladies. Later I realized that the self-diagnosis they were accusing me of was all about me figuring out that I had a milk allergy, which resulted in a special diet and setting myself apart from others. I was not at all convicted that any of these things were against God, but rather that the Bible tells us that God created the herbs for the service of man, for medicine and for our healing. I was not moving to their assault, fore I knew the Bible and my God lives inside of me. They became silent and after the young local minister tried to accuse me of losing my way when I purchased my land, which was so ridiculous, I countered him with the facts. They all became silent and left.

Proverbs 14:1 Every wise woman buildeth her house: but the foolish plucketh it down with her hands.

Psalms 104:14 He causeth the grass to grow for the cattle, and herb for the service of man: that he may bring forth food out of the earth;

Genesis 1:29 And God said, Behold, I have given you every herb bearing seed, which *is* upon the face of all the earth, and every tree, in the which *is* the fruit of a tree yielding seed; to you it shall be for meat.

Ezekiel 47:12 And by the river upon the bank thereof, on this side and on that side, shall grow all trees for meat, whose leaf shall not fade, neither shall the fruit thereof be consumed: it shall bring forth new fruit according to his months, because their waters they issued out of the sanctuary: and the fruit thereof shall be for meat, and the leaf thereof for medicine.

Hebrews 6:7 For the earth which drinketh in the rain that cometh oft upon it, and bringeth forth herbs meet for them by whom it is dressed, receiveth blessing from God:

Romans 14:2-3 For one believeth that he may eat all things: another, who is weak, eateth herbs. Let not him that eateth despise him that eateth not; and let not him which eateth not judge him that eateth: for God hath received him…..**Romans 14:13** Let us not therefore judge one another any more: but judge this rather, that no man put a stumblingblock or an occasion to fall in *his* brother's way….. **Romans 14:17** For the kingdom of God is not meat and drink; but

> righteousness, and peace, and joy in the Holy Ghost. **Colossians 2:16** Let no man therefore judge you in meat, or in drink, ...

After this encounter with these men I prayed for God to deliver me of the fear and He did this immediately. When the fear was gone the church's governing system crumbled. The fear is like the mortar and the manmade doctrines are like stones; the wall formed my prison, where I was dying. It was time for my Jesus to save me or else I would have died. So when I was delivered the walls of the prison collapsed to the ground, and there in front of me was my Lord illuminated. As I climbed out of the rubble, He took me into His arms and held me close. He wiped away the worry from my brow and kissed me. Then the healing began. With every lie He replaced it with scripture.

> **Colossians 2:8** Beware lest any man spoil you through philosophy and vain deceit, after the tradition of men, after the rudiments of the world, and not after Christ.

> **Matthew 15:9** But in vain they do worship me, teaching *for* doctrines the commandments of men.

> **Galatians 5:1** Stand fast therefore in the liberty wherewith Christ hath made us free, and be not entangled again with the yoke of bondage. **2:4** And that because of false brethren unawares brought in, who came in privily to spy out our liberty which we have in Christ

Jesus, that they might bring us into bondage: **5:4** Christ is become of no effect unto you, whosoever of you are justified by the law; ye are fallen from grace.

A significant part of the healing of my mind and body had to do with dispelling the fear. This religion is built around works, which they believe makes them the one true church. This belief sets them on high above all other so called Christians that they do not extend the handshake of fellowship to and cannot call them brothers. They do not believe one of their members can step down in rank and maintain your salvation. The scriptures following are the ones that put this belief system to shame.

Galatians 3:11-13 But that no man is justified by the law in the sight of God, *it is* evident: for, The just shall live by faith. And the law is not of faith: but, The man that doeth them shall live in them. Christ hath redeemed us from the curse of the law, being made a curse for us: for it is written, Cursed *is* every one that hangeth on a tree: **3:22** But the scripture hath concluded all under sin, that the promise by faith of Jesus Christ might be given to them that believe. **3:26-29** For ye are all the children of God by faith in Christ Jesus. For as many of you as have been baptized into Christ have put on Christ. There is neither Jew nor Greek, there is neither bond nor free, there is neither male nor female: for ye are all one in Christ Jesus. And if ye *be* Christ's, then are ye Abraham's seed, and heirs according to the promise.

Ephesians 2:8-9 For by grace are ye saved through faith; and that not of yourselves: *it is* the gift of God: Not of works, lest any man should boast. **Ephesians 2:15** Having abolished in his flesh the enmity, *even* the law of commandments *contained* in ordinances; for to make in himself of twain one new man, *so* making peace;

Romans 3:20-26 Therefore by the deeds of the law there shall no flesh be justified in his sight: for by the law *is* the knowledge of sin. But now the righteousness of God without the law is manifested, being witnessed by the law and the prophets; Even the righteousness of God *which is* by faith of Jesus Christ unto all and upon all them that believe: for there is no difference: For all have sinned, and come short of the glory of God; Being justified freely by his grace through the redemption that is in Christ Jesus: Whom God hath set forth *to be* a propitiation through faith in his blood, to declare his righteousness for the remission of sins that are past, through the forbearance of God; To declare, *I say*, at this time his righteousness: that he might be just, and the justifier of him which believeth in Jesus. **3:28-30** Therefore we conclude that a man is justified by faith without the deeds of the law. *Is he* the God of the Jews only? *is he* not also of the Gentiles? Yes, of the Gentiles also: Seeing *it is* one God, which shall justify the circumcision by faith, and uncircumcision through faith.

These scriptures were not hard for me to incorporate because I believe in Him and that the Bible is His Word infallible. Every time the devil would come to accuse me of not holding this or that church doctrine, Jesus would sweep me up and comfort me with a scripture that spoke to me perfectly on that particular accusation. Slowly by this method He healed my mind of the torment that comes from the fear of not measuring up to the dictations of men. He swept away all the government by which the group ruled their subjects. I knew the Bible, I had the Holy Spirit inside of me, and this was all I needed. I did not need men to govern me with their made up laws. It is not my desire to disobey God; neither do I desire the pleasures of sin, fore to me sin is not pleasure. The Bible says that if anyone adds to or takes away from the Bible that their names will be taken out of the book of life. This is just like in the days Jesus walked on earth. The Pharisees laid rules upon the people that they could not bear. This was not of God and He was so angry with them.

> **Matthew 16:11-12** How is it that ye do not understand that I spake *it* not to you concerning bread, that ye should beware of the leaven of the Pharisees and of the Sadducees? Then understood they how that he bade *them* not beware of the leaven of bread, but of the doctrine of the Pharisees and of the Sadducees.

> **1 John 2:26-27** These *things* have I written unto you concerning them that seduce you. But the anointing which ye have received of him abideth in you, and ye need not that any man teach you: but as the same anointing teacheth you of all things, and is truth, and is no lie, and even as it hath taught you, ye shall abide in him.

> **Matthew 23:1-38** Then spake Jesus to the multitude, and to his disciples, Saying, The scribes and the Pharisees sit in Moses' seat: All therefore whatsoever they bid you observe, *that* observe and do; but do not ye after their works: for they say, and do not. For they bind heavy burdens and grievous to be borne, and lay *them* on men's shoulders; but they *themselves* will not move them with one of their fingers. But all their works they do for to be seen of men: they make broad their phylacteries, and enlarge the borders of their garments, And love the uppermost rooms at feasts, and the chief seats in the synagogues, And greetings in the markets, and to be called of men, Rabbi, Rabbi. But be not ye called Rabbi: for one is your Master, *even*

Christ; and all ye are brethren. And call no *man* your father upon the earth: for one is your Father, which is in heaven. Neither be ye called masters: for one is your Master, *even* Christ. But he that is greatest among you shall be your servant. And whosoever shall exalt himself shall be abased; and he that shall humble himself shall be exalted. But woe unto you, scribes and Pharisees, hypocrites! for ye shut up the kingdom of heaven against men: for ye neither go in *yourselves*, neither suffer ye them that are entering to go in. Woe unto you, scribes and Pharisees, hypocrites! for ye devour widows' houses, and for a pretence make long prayer: therefore ye shall receive the greater damnation. Woe unto you, scribes and Pharisees, hypocrites! for ye compass sea and land to make one proselyte, and when he is made, ye make him twofold more the child of hell than yourselves. Woe unto you, *ye* blind guides, which say, Whosoever shall swear by the temple, it is nothing; but whosoever shall swear by the gold of the temple, he is a debtor! *Ye* fools and blind: for whether is greater, the gold, or the temple that sanctifieth the gold? And, Whosoever shall swear by the altar, it is nothing; but whosoever sweareth by the gift that is upon it, he is guilty. *Ye* fools and blind: for whether *is* greater, the gift, or the altar that sanctifieth the gift? Whoso therefore shall swear by the altar, sweareth by it, and by all things thereon. And whoso shall swear by the temple, sweareth by it, and by him that dwelleth therein. And he that shall swear by heaven, sweareth by the throne of God, and by him that sitteth thereon. Woe unto you, scribes and Pharisees, hypocrites! for ye pay tithe of mint and anise and cummin, and have omitted the weightier *matters* of the law, judgment, mercy, and faith: these ought ye to have done, and not to leave the other undone. *Ye* blind guides, which strain at a gnat, and swallow a camel. Woe unto you, scribes and Pharisees, hypocrites! for ye make clean the outside of the cup and of the platter, but within they are full of extortion and excess. *Thou* blind Pharisee, cleanse first that *which is* within the cup and platter, that the outside of them may be clean also. Woe unto you, scribes and Pharisees, hypocrites! for ye are like unto whited sepulchres, which indeed appear beautiful outward, but are within full of dead *men's* bones, and of all uncleanness. Even so ye also outwardly appear righteous unto men, but within ye are full of hypocrisy and iniquity. Woe unto you, scribes and Pharisees, hypocrites! because ye build the tombs of the prophets, and garnish the sepulchres of the righteous, And say, If we had been in the days of our fathers, we would not have been partakers with them in the blood of the prophets. Wherefore ye be witnesses unto yourselves, that ye are the children of them which killed the prophets. Fill ye up then the measure of your fathers. *Ye* serpents, *ye* generation of vipers, how can ye escape the damnation of hell? Wherefore, behold, I send unto you prophets, and wise men, and scribes: and *some* of them ye shall kill and crucify; and *some* of them shall ye scourge in your synagogues, and persecute *them* from city to city: That upon you may come all the righteous blood shed upon the earth, from the blood of righteous Abel unto the blood of Zacharias son of Barachias, whom ye slew between the temple and the altar. Verily I say unto you, All these things shall come upon this generation. O Jerusalem, Jerusalem, *thou* that killest the prophets, and stonest them which are sent unto thee, how often would I have gathered thy children together, even as a hen gathereth her chickens under *her* wings, and ye would not! Behold, your house is left unto you desolate.

The revivals continued with these two visiting ministers. They returned to our congregation for the third time. Winter was well advanced and after about two nights of meetings my horse fell sick. I doctored him around the clock. It was cold outside. The vet came out, said it was colic, gave him a shot and did not give me very much hope. I tried to keep him comfortable with continuous shots, but he was in severe pain. He was off feed and water. I tried to keep him walking as much as I could, until finally he just could not walk any more. In the barn under the roof he spent his last hours rising to his feet, and then laying back down. He would moan and moan. He pawed the walls and the feeder, then lie back down and moan. It was heart-breaking to watch. He was my Buddy. I had to keep taking breaks to warm up and try to sleep a bit. With my adrenal condition all these factors were against me, the cold, no sleep, and the incredible grief watching my Buddy suffer. A few of the neighbors came to give me a bit of a break so I could rest. But for the long haul it was me and Buddy, then after forty eight hours came the final moment. I was at the house where I listened to his constant pawing at the barn wall. Then there was a silence. It was in the early morning, still darkish. I pulled on my warm clothes and went to the barn where I could see him laying there, not moving. I walked up to him, touched his lifeless body and cried. My Buddy was gone: gone from me forever. He was such a good horse, never did anything mean, and always took me for a gentle ride along the creek or up the mountain. He was strong, steady and kind, I loved him. I walked away from my friend, never to kiss him on his nose again.

At the house I waited until most people are awake then made a phone call to a Mennonite family and told them my sad story. I was going to try and find a backhoe in the neighborhood, but this man told me he would take care of it. So he got a relative to come with a backhoe. I just stayed in the house and they buried him. I was thankful for this. These kinds of things are very hard for me.

I was very exhausted from the trauma and yet I attended church right away, as revivals had just started and would go nightly for about two weeks. Every member is expected to attend as it is an effort to bring every person to see their sins and repent so they can go to communion with a clear conscience. Communion is the goal. I remember telling one sister what happened to my horse. I had missed a few meetings and was about to miss a bunch more. After two days I collapsed. My adrenals failed. I know only a minute or two before I am completely unable to move, so I grabbed the phone and called the neighbor, asking her to come quickly. I also called my son, Lew. I was losing feeling fast. My whole body becomes numb. He had been with me during previous incidents and had learned what to do to keep me alive. Lew's home was about a forty five minute drive from my house. By the time anyone arrived I could not move my body anymore. I was lying flat out on the couch. My neighbor did not know what to do. I could barely whisper in syllables. When Lew arrived he took over, got the cortisol under my tongue, mixed up an electrolyte drink with added salt, and with a crimped straw got me to drink. He pushed the drinks and kept adding cortisol under my tongue. The neighbor lady's husband showed up hours later and together with Lew they carried me to the bathroom. I was at least able to balance there for a minute, and then they carried me back to the couch. I was seven hours in this state, coming out slowly until I could walk with help to the bathroom. My son Lew stayed beside me the whole night until he was confident he could leave me to go and lay down. He set an alarm to get up every two hours to check me. This was truly love. I needed his love.

To say the least I was bed-ridden for many days and missed revival meetings except for the last day, when the congregation went to communion. I was not a candidate for communion because I did not examine myself through the course of the meetings. So on communion night I sat on the back row with some other ladies who were also not taking communion. Though I knew the Lord was with me, I was where He wanted me, was freer than ever before since I had been delivered of the fear and repented of all the man made doctrines. I could sing with gusto the song called, "It is Well With My Soul".

I marveled that the home ministers could go to communion with a clear conscience, but they did go. The Bible says that if you take communion unworthily you are guilty of the blood of Christ and bring damnation upon yourself. I wondered later if God so chose to take my horse at the time He did, to spare me of partaking of communion with these men who claimed they were free.

It was right in the middle of this series of revivals that my older son, Jim, was homeless, sick, hungry, and destitute. He was living in his car that was piled to the ceiling with everything he owned. He called me for help. Over recent months his contacts with me were the first in seven years. I love my sons and those seven years were heart-breaking to me; one of those oppressive situations that drag a person down.

But the Mennonite ministers were sayin', "Don't help your son!" This did not feel right to me and God was giving me scriptures to the contrary.

> **Luke 3:11** He answereth and saith unto them, He that hath two coats, let him impart to him that hath none; and he that hath meat, let him do likewise.

> **Matthew 7:7-12** Ask, and it shall be given you; seek, and ye shall find; knock, and it shall be opened unto you: For every one that asketh receiveth; and he that seeketh findeth; and to him that knocketh it shall be opened. Or what man is there of you, whom if his son ask bread, will he give him a stone? Or if he ask a fish, will he give him a serpent? If ye then, being evil, know how to give good gifts unto your children, how much more shall your Father which is in heaven give good things to them that ask him? Therefore all things whatsoever

ye would that men should do to you, do ye even so to them: for this is the law and the prophets.

Matthew 5:41-42 And whosoever shall compel thee to go a mile, go with him twain. Give to him that asketh thee, and from him that would borrow of thee turn not thou away.

Matthew 25:34-46 Then shall the King say unto them on his right hand, Come, ye blessed of my Father, inherit the kingdom prepared for you from the foundation of the world: For I was an hungred, and ye gave me meat: I was thirsty, and ye gave me drink: I was a stranger, and ye took me in: Naked, and ye clothed me: I was sick, and ye visited me: I was in prison, and ye came unto me. Then shall the righteous answer him, saying, Lord, when saw we thee an hungred, and fed *thee*? or thirsty, and gave *thee* drink? When saw we thee a stranger, and took *thee* in? or naked, and clothed *thee*? Or when saw we thee sick, or in prison, and came unto thee? And the King shall answer and say unto them, Verily I say unto you, Inasmuch as ye have done *it* unto one of the least of these my brethren, ye have done *it* unto me. Then shall he say also unto them on the left hand, Depart from me, ye cursed, into everlasting fire, prepared for the devil and his angels: For I was an hungred, and ye gave me no meat: I was thirsty, and ye gave me no drink: I was a stranger, and ye took me not in: naked, and ye clothed me not: sick, and in prison, and ye visited me not. Then shall they also answer him, saying, Lord, when saw we thee an hungred, or athirst, or a stranger, or naked, or sick, or in prison, and did not minister unto thee? Then shall he answer them, saying, Verily I say unto you, Inasmuch as ye did *it* not to one of the least of these, ye did *it* not to me. And these shall go away into everlasting punishment: but the righteous into life eternal.

Deliverance from Oppression

These are only a few of the scriptures that the Lord was bringing to me constantly. A month passed and my son was still living in his car in the Wal-Mart parking lot, without even a place to lie down, because the car was piled full to the ceiling. Finally I asked him to decide what he wanted to do: stay there or drive back to our town and see if he could find work there. He decided to come back to our home town, so I gave him gas money. It was at that time the older minister decided to call me after no communication for two weeks and asked how my son was getting along. I told him he was right then driving back here. He just said, "I see, well okay," and hung up. Ten minutes later the young minister calls up and said, "We told you not to help your son!" I tried to explain but he was hot and yelling. I had it with their control and manipulation. I hung up on him. That marked the end of letting them walk all over me and control my life above and beyond the leading of God. It was shortly later that I was delivered of fear. God instilled in me a strength from on high to stand my ground. I was no longer afraid of what man could do to me. Their judgment was of men, not of God. I had, had it! In later phone conversations I laid it all out to them both, the acts that they had committed toward me and how damaging these things were. I left no stone un-turned. I told them, "I'm done". I don't think they knew then what I was talking about but they soon did.

25.

FIND A DOCTOR

Finally I decided that I had to see a doctor who specialized in adrenal disease. So I made my appointment, he ordered tests and was shocked at the condition of my adrenals. I was choking on my food, had no gag reflex and no feeling in the back of my throat. No medical doctor was able to figure that one out. He immediately said that the throat was controlled by the Sympathetic Nervous System. This nervous system was controlled by the adrenals. I thought it might be Amyotrophic Lateral Sclerosis because my brother died of that. The first set of muscle control that he lost was his throat and gag reflex. My doctor put me on an adequate dose of hydrocortisone and within two weeks my gag reflex was back. I no longer was choking on my food. I remain on this dose today and I still have a gag reflex. My doctor says I could be on cortisol replacement for life because of the extensive damage to my adrenals. There are some supplements to build up the adrenal gland but because of limited income I cannot afford all that I need. I do everything I can to stay healthy, eat well, and I have chosen to eliminate my sources of stress. The detriments of this disease are very complex. I won't explain it all. For anyone suffering this malady

I suggest you read and study about adrenal fatigue, there are many good reference books out today, written by doctors. Search for them and search for a doctor who knows how to treat this condition.

Shortly hereafter I decided I was done with the church group. If I was to recover from this malady I would have to provide for myself a stress-free environment as best as I could. One cannot live in fear, which triggers the "fight and flight" response, which in turn a constant demand for adrenaline/cortisol production; and live very long.

I will not divulge all the many incidents of the persecution I suffered. I only want to portray a bit so if any other person is living under such things and chooses to continue for long periods of time, I hope to encourage you to reconsider the circumstances. Sometimes it looks like there is no way of escape. Oppression can become a way of life that is accepted. We take the abuse and swallow it. Then we take more and swallow it. But it burns inside the heart and the gut. It permeates the fibers of our being. We accept that there are no answers and we endure, but we really aren't enduring. We are dying inside our soul and our body. We lose our person, our worth to mankind and seemingly to God. And if we are delivered from this demon, recovery can be very long. Our mind has to be reprogrammed with Truth. Truth will set us free.

Maybe some people say that if you have a strong relationship with God the affects may be minimal from someone who is beating you, or verbally assaulting you daily, or ensnares you with coercion. This may be true to some degree. But more likely than not you could be bodily harmed and perhaps killed. I think certain personalities are more easily adapted to let things roll off their back like water on a duck's back, and with God we can do all things through Him who strengthens us. But I really don't think it is profitable for anyone to live under abuse. If children are involved, their lives could be affected permanently. With young children in the formative years, if they are held in an environment of trauma and terror, the frontal lobe of the brain does not develop and they only activate the part of the brain that integrates survival. I explain it this way: the frontal lobe is where the human emotions develop like love, trust, hope, safety, and so on. The survival instincts are like any animal would have intact-how to stay alive. Humans learn manipulation, controlling the environment around them so they are assured no one else is in control that could endanger their lives. Getting food and essentials can be implemented in ways we would see unnecessary since there is lots of food available and served regularly. Survival is all they know and it may not make any sense to those around them. This illness is called Attachment Disorder. Sometimes in severe cases it is called Reactive Attachment Disorder. These children grow up and cannot trust. Love is foreign to them. To attach to a family member, especially the mother who did not keep them safe, is almost impossible. Methods are being implemented today to try to alter these cases to activate the frontal lobe of the brain, but the best efforts may not show a lot of change. If the condition is caught at an early age some success can be hoped for. There are some success stories, but this has only been recognized and understood in recent years. Let's pray for the children and those who have grown up already with this condition.

26.

FALSE TEACHING

Some of the tactics and claims of this religious group of which I was a member for twenty two years, are quite common among cults. The reason I want to lift out these things is for educational purposes, not for revenge. I am not an authority in these issues, only one who has experienced cult practices. I want to help others to see and recognize these things as extra-Biblical, implemented of men, and not of God. We are not called to follow men, but to follow God. That does not mean that men should never be an example for us to look to. The apostles Peter and Paul held himself out as an example of one following Christ.

> **1 Peter 5:3** Neither as being lords over *God's* heritage, but being ensamples to the flock.

I think in his day this was a much-needed tool because there was so much deception and the Christian faith was just in its infancy. Proud men who loved the power that perhaps they could gain over people were looking for their opportunity to gain a following. We still encounter such men and religions today. I can only speak from my own personal experience in what I saw and became victim of. And again I take the responsibility of my own victimization due to weakness and deception. I chose to allow these men to control and manipulate my life to my own destruction. But the destruction that God allowed to happen to me was the factor that woke me from my stupor. I can say with honesty today that I am eternally grateful to God for allowing me to come to near death and the end of my finances; that I was desperate enough to look beyond men and into the eyes of God and find my deliverance.

Please beware of all organizations that claim they are the one true church on earth. To leave it is the same as leaving God and is an automatic going-to-hell sentence. This is highly coercive and a fear inducing tactic, and even though it may be believed by the leaders, and even those who imposed this belief system generations before, this does not make it true. The Bible says all who "believe" in Jesus and who He was: the Son of God, the Son of man, and what He did to save us once and for all, if we repent of our sins and accept His sacrifice for the forgiveness of sin on the cross; we are saved, are the saints, the body, the church, the bride. I direct all to the Word of God and to seek His Holy Spirit to lead you into all truth.

> **John 16:13** Howbeit when he, the Spirit of truth, is come, he will guide you into all truth: for he shall not speak of himself; but whatsoever he shall hear, *that* shall he speak: and he will shew you things to come.

> **Romans 1:16** For I am not ashamed of the gospel of Christ: for it is the power of God unto salvation to every one that believeth; to the Jew first, and also to the Greek.

Romans 12:5 So we, *being* many, are one body in Christ, and every one members one of another.

Ephesians 1:13 In whom ye also *trusted*, after that ye heard the word of truth, the gospel of your salvation: in whom also after that ye believed, ye were sealed with that holy Spirit of promise,

Ephesians 5:30-33 For we are members of his body, of his flesh, and of his bones. For this cause shall a man leave his father and mother, and shall be joined unto his wife, and they two shall be one flesh. This is a great mystery: but I speak concerning Christ and the church. Nevertheless let every one of you in particular so love his wife even as himself; and the wife *see* that she reverence *her* husband.

Acts 13:39 And by him all that believe are justified from all things, from which ye could not be justified by the law of Moses.

John 6:40 And this is the will of him that sent me, that every one which seeth the Son, and believeth on him, may have everlasting life: and I will raise him up at the last day.

1 Corinthians 1:2 Unto the church of God which is at Corinth, to them that are sanctified in Christ Jesus, called *to be* saints, with all that in every place call upon the name of Jesus Christ our Lord, both theirs and ours: **12:27** Now ye are the body of Christ, and members in particular.

Colossians 1:18-24 And he is the head of the body, the church: who is the beginning, the firstborn from the dead; that in all *things* he might have the preeminence. For it pleased *the Father* that in him should all fulness dwell; And, having made peace through the blood of his cross, by him to reconcile all things unto himself; by him, *I say*, whether *they be* things in earth, or things in heaven. And you, that were sometime alienated and enemies in *your* mind by wicked works, yet now hath he reconciled In the body of his flesh through death, to present you holy and unblameable and unreproveable in his sight: If ye continue in the faith grounded and settled, and *be* not moved away from the hope of the gospel, which ye have heard, *and* which was preached to every creature which is under heaven; whereof I Paul am made a minister; Who now rejoice in my sufferings for you, and fill up that which is behind of the afflictions of Christ in my flesh for his body's sake, which is the church:

Romans 3:19-26 Now we know that what things soever the law saith, it saith to them who are under the law: that every mouth may be stopped, and all the world may become guilty before God. Therefore by the deeds of the law there shall no flesh be justified in his sight: for by the law *is* the knowledge of sin. But now the righteousness of God without the law is manifested, being witnessed by the law and the prophets; Even the righteousness of God *which is* by faith of Jesus Christ unto all and upon all them that believe: for there is no difference: For all have sinned, and come short of the glory of God; Being justified freely by his grace through the redemption that is in Christ Jesus: Whom God hath set forth *to be* a propitiation through faith in his blood, to declare his righteousness for the remission of sins that are past, through the forbearance of God; To declare, *I say*, at this time his righteousness: that he might be just, and the justifier of him which believeth in Jesus.

Romans 10:9-13 That if thou shalt confess with thy mouth the Lord Jesus, and shalt believe in thine heart that God hath raised him from the dead, thou shalt be saved. For with the heart man believeth unto righteousness; and with the mouth confession is made unto salvation. For the scripture saith, Whosoever believeth on him shall not be ashamed. For there is no difference between the Jew and the Greek: for the same Lord over all is rich unto all that call upon him. For whosoever shall call upon the name of the Lord shall be saved.

Galatians 3:22 But the scripture hath concluded all under sin, that the promise by faith of Jesus Christ might be given to them that believe. **3:26-29** For ye are all the children of God by faith in Christ Jesus. For as many of you as have been baptized into Christ have put on Christ. There is neither Jew nor Greek, there is neither bond nor free, there is neither male nor female: for ye are all one in Christ Jesus. And if ye *be* Christ's, then are ye Abraham's seed, and heirs according to the promise.

Matthew 25:10 And while they went to buy, the bridegroom came; and they that were ready went in with him to the marriage: and the door was shut.

Revelation 21:9 And there came unto me one of the seven angels which had the seven vials full of the seven last plagues, and talked with me, saying, Come hither, I will shew thee the bride, the Lamb's wife.

1 Corinthians 1:2 Unto the church of God which is at Corinth, to them that are sanctified in Christ Jesus, called *to be* saints, with all that in every place call upon the name of Jesus Christ our Lord, both theirs and ours:

False Teaching

The point I am hoping to lift out here is that all men who believe in Jesus Christ, no matter who you are; become part of the family of God; are part of His body, the church; considered a brother, a saint; His bride; and are a recipient of His Holy Spirit. The reward is the same as all who are saved and that is life in eternity with the Father, Jesus and the Holy Spirit. God is no respecter of persons. There are no elite groups. When we are saved we are His, grafted in to the Vine, which is Christ Jesus.

> **John 15:5** I am the vine, ye *are* the branches: He that abideth in me, and I in him, the same bringeth forth much fruit: for without me ye can do nothing.

> **Romans 11:13-25** For I speak to you Gentiles, inasmuch as I am the apostle of the Gentiles, I magnify mine office: If by any means I may provoke to emulation *them which are* my flesh, and might save some of them. For if the casting away of them *be* the reconciling of the world, what *shall* the receiving *of them be*, but life from the dead? For if the firstfruit *be* holy, the lump *is* also *holy*: and if the root *be* holy, so *are* the branches. And if some of the branches be broken off, and thou, being a wild olive tree, wert graffed in among them, and with them partakest of the root and fatness of the olive tree; Boast not against the branches. But if thou boast, thou bearest not the root, but the root thee. Thou wilt say then, The branches were broken off, that I might be graffed in. Well; because of unbelief they were broken off, and thou standest by faith. Be not highminded, but fear: For if God spared not the natural branches, *take heed* lest he also spare not thee. Behold therefore the goodness and severity of God: on them which fell, severity; but toward thee, goodness, if thou continue in *his* goodness: otherwise thou also shalt be cut off. And they also, if

they abide not still in unbelief, shall be graffed in: for God is able to graff them in again. For if thou wert cut out of the olive tree which is wild by nature, and wert graffed contrary to nature into a good olive tree: how much more shall these, which be the natural *branches*, be graffed into their own olive tree? For I would not, brethren, that ye should be ignorant of this mystery, lest ye should be wise in your own conceits; that blindness in part is happened to Israel, until the fulness of the Gentiles be come in.

Romans 12:5 So we, *being* many, are one body in Christ, and every one members one of another.

Ephesians 5:30 For we are members of his body, of his flesh, and of his bones. **5:32** This is a great mystery: but I speak concerning Christ and the church.

Acts 2:47 Praising God, and having favour with all the people. And the Lord added to the church daily such as should be saved.

More dangers of false doctrine: when a group lifts themselves up as the chosen ones above all others and claims the position of "Israel", beware. This is called "replacement theology". The above scripture teaches us that Israel is considered to God as the good olive tree and the Gentiles are like the wild olive branches that are grafted into the good olive tree. When we get grafted in we dare not boast lest we get cut off and cast into the fire. If you understand the Bible, it is a mystery why Israel was blinded in part for a season so the Gentiles could be saved. In the Old Testament, heathen nations, or the Gentiles, so to speak, were forbidden for Israel to make marriages with, that they would not be influenced by idol worship. But when Jesus came He broke down the barriers by His shed blood. Salvation was provided for all mankind. We are His creation and He made the Holy Spirit available to all. By this avenue we all, Greek and Jew alike, can become like Him, in Him: His very own children, His bride. Let us not exalt ourselves above others because we think by our works of righteousness, we are more favored by Him. When God sees the saved He sees the blood, not our dress or our hair or our mowed lawn. To think we can grant favor by our works is quite dangerous. And by our works of righteousness does not make a Greek, a Jew.

> **Galatians 5:4** Christ is become of no effect unto you, whosoever of you are justified by the law; ye are fallen from grace.

> **Acts 10:28** And he said unto them, Ye know how that it is an unlawful thing for a man that is a Jew to keep company, or come unto one of another nation; but God hath shewed me that I should not call any man common or unclean. **10:34-35** Then Peter opened *his* mouth, and said, Of a truth I perceive that God is no respecter of persons: But in every nation he that feareth him, and worketh righteousness, is accepted with him.

This belief system that their group is the only one true church leads into many veins of deception. It gives the leaders power to control and manipulate its members, all under the guise of directing that one into Heaven with God. This is where the brainwashing comes in. There is much propaganda that goes into effect. Think for a moment about how Hitler brainwashed millions of people to come under his rule and thinking. He started repeating his doctrine over loudspeakers in the streets and in the schools, starting out the children at a young age. It was all lies and it took the repeating of his doctrine over and over and over again until it became a part of the makeup of each brain that took it in. Only the strong morally could stand against this brainwashing. Now think of this method implicated in cults. The leaders present a doctrine and bring in aspects of that doctrine from all angles. It is repeated by the members to each other and examples are brought forth constantly. For example the doctrine that feeds the strength of the "one true church" belief; that all who leave this church whether by choice or by the church expelling them; are lost and going to hell if they do not repent and return to the church. It is often observed that these expelled ones go on to live immoral lives. This is held as evidence that those who leave are lost, or so it is perceived when you live within the confines of this belief system. But from the outside standing in the Light, it becomes obvious that many who leave the confines of these cults have not God in their hearts to start with and are no more empowered to obey the Word of God than the sinner on the streets. When they are inside the confines of the church they are governed by fear and the power of coercion. They are held in a ridged life style by fear of going to hell. They are consoled by their outward appearance that they are right with God.

Another aspect of deception that brings the people of these religious groups to fear and tremble at the demands and manipulation of their leaders is that they say that one cannot trust their own light, but only the light of the brethren. Another words, a person is not to trust the leading of the Holy Spirit in their own life, but rather the Holy Spirit in your brother's lives. The scripture that they stand on is this: **Proverbs 11:14** Where no counsel *is*, the people fall: but in the multitude of counsellers *there is* safety. There is truth in this scripture; if God does not provide counsel to a man he can look to other Christians to help prove a matter. But when it is taken so far as to say that the voice of the church is the same as the voice of God and to disobey is the same as disobeying God, approaches very dangerous ground. This puts the church as infallible and supreme in its government of men's lives. It puts the church in the place of God; this is a clear distinction of a cult, not a church of the true God. In this belief system a man is forbidden to question the church or suggest any fallibility of their doctrines. Beware my friend if you find yourself under such mandates.

> **Psalms 118:8-9** *It is* better to trust in the LORD than to put confidence in man. *It is* better to trust in the LORD than to put confidence in princes.

> **Matthew 20:25-28** But Jesus called them *unto him*, and said, Ye know that the princes of the Gentiles exercise dominion over them, and they that are great exercise authority upon them. But it shall not be so among you: but whosoever will be great among you, let him be your minister; And whosoever will be chief among you, let him be your servant: Even as the Son of man came not to be ministered unto, but to minister, and to give his life a ransom for many.

> **1 John 2:27** But the anointing which ye have received of him abideth in you, and ye need not that any man teach you: but as the same anointing teacheth you of all things, and is truth, and is no lie, and even as it hath taught you, ye shall abide in him.

When a person is indoctrinated to such beliefs as described above they will not listen to anyone who would dare to contradict their doctrines. To them this would be the same as listening to the devil. They would fear that to even listen they might be weakened and fall from the way. Again fear has them imprisoned to the point of near impossibility of escape. A brainwashed person is hard to reach.

Acts 28:26-27 Saying, Go unto this people, and say, Hearing ye shall hear, and shall not understand; and seeing ye shall see, and not perceive: For the heart of this people is waxed gross, and their ears are dull of hearing, and their eyes have they closed; lest they should see with *their* eyes, and hear with *their* ears, and understand with *their* heart, and should be converted, and I should heal them.

Jeremiah 2:13 For my people have committed two evils; they have forsaken me the fountain of living waters, *and* hewed them out cisterns, broken cisterns, that can hold no water.

Jeremiah 5:3-4 O LORD, *are* not thine eyes upon the truth? thou hast stricken them, but they have not grieved; thou hast consumed them, *but* they have refused to receive correction: they have made their faces harder than a rock; they have refused to return. Therefore I said, Surely these *are* poor; they are foolish: for they know not the way of the LORD, *nor* the judgment of their God.

Zechariah 7:11 But they refused to hearken, and pulled away the shoulder, and stopped their ears, that they should not hear.

Matthew 13:15 For this people's heart is waxed gross, and *their* ears are dull of hearing, and their eyes they have closed; lest at any time they should see with *their* eyes, and hear with *their* ears, and should understand with *their* heart, and should be converted, and I should heal them.

Job 41:24 His heart is as firm as a stone; yea, as hard as a piece of the nether *millstone*.

27.

Who is the Messiah?

Believing in Jesus: that word believing takes in the entire person of God the Son incarnate. This means that God the Son actually became human taking on real flesh and blood. The Bible clearly teaches us that He, the Messiah, would come from the linage of Judah, speaking clearly that He would come from the seed of mankind. The Word of God lists some names of actual people on earth that from their seed-the reproductive seed of man-would come the Messiah. To not believe this is to not believe in Jesus. Here are the scriptures that tell us plainly:

> **John 8:24** I said therefore unto you, that ye shall die in your sins: for if ye believe not that I am *he*, ye shall die in your sins.

> **Genesis 3:15** And I will put enmity between thee and the woman, and between thy seed and her seed; it shall bruise thy head, and thou shalt bruise his heel.

Genesis 22:15-18 And the angel of the LORD called unto Abraham out of heaven the second time, And said, By myself have I sworn, saith the LORD, for because thou hast done this thing, and hast not withheld thy son, thine only *son*: That in blessing I will bless thee, and in multiplying I will multiply thy seed as the stars of the heaven, and as the sand which *is* upon the sea shore; and thy seed shall possess the gate of his enemies; And in thy seed shall all the nations of the earth be blessed; because thou hast obeyed my voice.

Genesis 49:10 The sceptre shall not depart from Judah, nor a lawgiver from between his feet, until Shiloh come; and unto him *shall* the gathering of the people *be*.

Hebrews 2:16 For verily he took not on *him the nature of* angels; but he took on *him* the seed of Abraham.

Psalms 132:11 The LORD hath sworn *in* truth unto David; he will not turn from it; Of the fruit of thy body will I set upon thy throne.

Isaiah 11:1-10 And there shall come forth a rod out of the stem of Jesse, and a Branch shall grow out of his roots: And the spirit of the LORD shall rest upon him, the spirit of wisdom and understanding, the spirit of counsel and might, the spirit of knowledge and of the fear of the LORD; And shall make him of quick understanding in the fear of the LORD: and he shall not judge after the sight of his eyes, neither reprove after the hearing of his ears: But with righteousness shall he judge the poor, and reprove with equity for the meek of the earth: and he shall smite the earth with the rod of his mouth, and with the breath of his lips shall he slay the wicked. And righteousness shall be the girdle of his loins, and faithfulness the girdle of his reins. The wolf also shall dwell with the lamb, and the leopard shall lie down with the kid; and the calf and the young lion and the fatling together; and a little child shall lead them. And the cow and the bear shall feed; their young ones shall lie down together: and the lion shall eat straw like the ox. And the sucking child shall play on the hole of the asp, and the weaned child shall put his hand on the cockatrice' den. They shall not hurt nor destroy in all my holy mountain: for the earth shall be full of the knowledge of the LORD, as the waters cover the sea. And in that day there shall be a root of Jesse, which shall stand for an ensign of the people; to it shall the Gentiles seek: and his rest shall be glorious.

Revelation 22:16 I Jesus have sent mine angel to testify unto you these things in the churches. I am the root and the offspring of David, *and* the bright and morning star.

Acts 2:29-30 Men *and* brethren, let me freely speak unto you of the patriarch David, that he is both dead and buried, and his sepulchre is with us unto this day. Therefore being a prophet, and knowing that God had sworn with an oath to him, that of the fruit of his loins, according to the flesh, he would raise up Christ to sit on his throne;

Romans 1:3-4 Concerning his Son Jesus Christ our Lord, which was made of the seed of David according to the flesh; And declared *to be* the Son of God with power, according to the spirit of holiness, by the resurrection from the dead:

Galatians 4:4 But when the fulness of the time was come, God sent forth his Son, made of a woman, made under the law,

> **John 1:14** And the Word was made flesh, and dwelt among us, (and we beheld his glory, the glory as of the only begotten of the Father,) full of grace and truth.

> **Hosea 5:14** For I *will be* unto Ephraim as a lion, and as a young lion to the house of Judah: I, *even* I, will tear and go away; I will take away, and none shall rescue *him*.

> **Revelation 5:5** And one of the elders saith unto me, Weep not: behold, the Lion of the tribe of Juda, the Root of David, hath prevailed to open the book, and to loose the seven seals thereof.

These are only a few scriptures that tell us that He, the Son of God, came to earth, took the actual seed of man, and was born of a woman to become the Messiah, the Lamb of God.

Then there are those groups or cults that do not believe He was divine. Another words, they do not believe that He was the only begotten Son of the Father, God Almighty, or that He was one of the Godhead and one with the Father. Some cults say He was just a created angel like Michael, Lucifer, and Gabriel. Here are a few scriptures to show us clearly He is one with the Father, only a separate manifestation. That He is the ONLY BEGOTTEN SON OF GOD:

> **Revelation 4:8** And the four beasts had each of them six wings about *him*; and *they were* full of eyes within: and they rest not day and night, saying, Holy, holy, holy, Lord God Almighty, which was, and is, and is to come.

Revelation 1:8 I am Alpha and Omega, the beginning and the ending, saith the Lord, which is, and which was, and which is to come, the Almighty.

1 Timothy 3:16 And without controversy great is the mystery of godliness: God was manifest in the flesh, justified in the Spirit, seen of angels, preached unto the Gentiles, believed on in the world, received up into glory.

Genesis 35:10-13 And God said unto him, Thy name *is* Jacob: thy name shall not be called any more Jacob, but Israel shall be thy name: and he called his name Israel. And God said unto him, I *am* God Almighty: be fruitful and multiply; a nation and a company of nations shall be of thee, and kings shall come out of thy loins; And the land which I gave Abraham and Isaac, to thee I will give it, and to thy seed after thee will I give the land. And God went up from him in the place where he talked with him. (Take note that no man hath seen the Father at any time)

1 John 4:12 No man hath seen God at any time. If we love one another, God dwelleth in us, and his love is perfected in us.

John 5:37 And the Father himself, which hath sent me, hath borne witness of me. Ye have neither heard his voice at any time, nor seen his shape.

John 6:46 Not that any man hath seen the Father, save he which is of God, he hath seen the Father.

Isaiah 9:6 For unto us a child is born, unto us a son is given: and the government shall be upon his shoulder: and his name shall be called Wonderful, Counsellor, The mighty God, The everlasting Father, The Prince of Peace.

John 14:10-11 Believest thou not that I am in the Father, and the Father in me? the words that I speak unto you I speak not of myself: but the Father that dwelleth in me, he doeth the works. Believe me that I *am* in the Father, and the Father in me: or else believe me for the very works' sake.

To disbelieve in who Jesus was and is, is of antichrist. Therefore such religious groups or cults that deny Jesus' true identity are presenting another Jesus. Antichrist was in the world in the Bible days. We were warned that this spirit would be here on earth unto the last days and then the Antichrist embodied will arise to rule the whole earth. Let us not be deceived who is the true Christ.

2 John 1:7 For many deceivers are entered into the world, who confess not that Jesus Christ is come in the flesh. This is a deceiver and an antichrist.

1 John 2:22 Who is a liar but he that denieth that Jesus is the Christ? He is antichrist, that denieth the Father and the Son.

Clearly there are many churches that are not of Christ Jesus even if they claim His name. They are led of other spirits posing as God. I hope that with all these scriptures the reader can discern that there will be many false prophets, false teachers and spirits that will attempt to lead us astray. May we all study the Word, humbly submit to Christ, and beware, a watchman on the wall; for the deceiver, which is Satan, goeth about to destroy and rob God of His lambs, disguising himself in many ways.

> **Matthew 7:15** Beware of false prophets, which come to you in sheep's clothing, but inwardly they are ravening wolves.

> **Matthew 24:24** For there shall arise false Christs, and false prophets, and shall shew great signs and wonders; insomuch that, if *it were* possible, they shall deceive the very elect.

> **2 Peter 2:1** But there were false prophets also among the people, even as there shall be false teachers among you, who privily shall bring in damnable heresies, even denying the Lord that bought them, and bring upon themselves swift destruction.

Please study the book of Revelation to be able to recognize the coming Antichrist, who will be Satan embodied, who will rise up to rule the world, calling himself God and sitting on the seat of God in His temple.

> **2 Thessalonians 2:2-4** That ye be not soon shaken in mind, or be troubled, neither by spirit, nor by word, nor by letter as from us, as that the day of Christ is at hand. Let no man deceive you by any means: for *that day shall not come*, except there come a falling away first, and that man of sin be revealed, the son of perdition; Who opposeth and exalteth himself above all that is called God, or that is worshipped; so that he as God sitteth in the temple of God, shewing himself that he is God.

Revelation 13:1-9 And I stood upon the sand of the sea, and saw a beast rise up out of the sea, having seven heads and ten horns, and upon his horns ten crowns, and upon his heads the name of blasphemy. And the beast which I saw was like unto a leopard, and his feet were as *the feet* of a bear, and his mouth as the mouth of a lion: and the dragon gave him his power, and his seat, and great authority. And I saw one of his heads as it were wounded to death; and his deadly wound was healed: and all the world wondered after the beast. And they worshipped the dragon which gave power unto the beast: and they worshipped the beast, saying, Who *is* like unto the beast? who is able to make war with him? And there was given unto him a mouth speaking great things and blasphemies; and power was given unto him to continue forty *and* two months. And he opened his mouth in blasphemy against God, to blaspheme his name, and his tabernacle, and them that dwell in heaven. And it was given unto him to make war with the saints, and to overcome them: and power was given him over all kindreds, and tongues, and nations. And all that dwell upon the earth shall worship him, whose names are not written in the book of life of the Lamb slain from the foundation of the world. If any man have an ear, let him hear.

Revelation 14:9-12 And the third angel followed them, saying with a loud voice, If any man worship the beast and his image, and receive *his* mark in his forehead, or in his hand, The same shall drink of the wine of the wrath of God, which is poured out without mixture into the cup of his indignation; and he shall be tormented with fire and brimstone in the presence of the holy angels, and in the presence of the Lamb: And the smoke of their torment ascendeth up for ever and ever: and they have no rest day nor night, who worship the beast and his image, and whosoever receiveth the mark of his name. Here is the patience of the saints: here *are* they that keep the commandments of God, and the faith of Jesus.

Dear friends we are in the last days. If you or I are not taken up in the rapture of the saints, and we live through the many plagues that will befall the earth, we will see the Antichrist rise. Study the Word of God and be watching that you be not deceived, fore he will perform signs and miracles, calling himself God and will deceive many. It will be mandated by this Antichrist, for all to receive a mark, either in their head or right hand. The Bible warns us, if we receive the mark we will be cast into the lake of fire. Take heed my friend, only by Jesus can any man stand in those days.

28.

GET HELP

After the characteristics of cults, consider the repercussions of living long in an abusive and oppressive situation and what that can do to our health, and sometimes our mental stability. Foremost let us all look to Jesus for our healing. He can erase the lies and replace them with truth. And He works supernaturally in our mind and heart. But I have found it takes time. Friends are a blessing to share with what we are going through. Talk with other Christians and perhaps you will find some who have come out of spiritual oppression that can comfort and strengthen you. There is hope for healing; do not condemn yourself. Move forward, let your emotions out and realize it is a natural human emotion to be angry that you could have been so deceived, or robbed, or subject to declining health because of long term fear and trauma. Jesus forgives us. Just tell Him all about it, be sorry, take hold of His hand, and let Him lead you beside the still waters.

If you are stuck and need professional help there are lots of Christian psychologists and other skilled counselors that can help lead you out of the rubble. Do not feel guilty. Just keep moving forward. Believe in His Holy Word and be strong against the faces of those who will no doubt

Get Help

be accusing you of leaving God. Take your sins to Jesus and have faith in His shed blood to wash your sins away.

> **Ezekiel 3:8-9** Behold, I have made thy face strong against their faces, and thy forehead strong against their foreheads. As an adamant harder than flint have I made thy forehead: fear them not, neither be dismayed at their looks, though they *be* a rebellious house.

> **Micah 7:18-19** Who *is* a God like unto thee, that pardoneth iniquity, and passeth by the transgression of the remnant of his heritage? he retaineth not his anger for ever, because he delighteth *in* mercy. He will turn again, he will have compassion upon us; he will subdue our iniquities; and thou wilt cast all their sins into the depths of the sea.

Remember you are special to God.

> **Luke 12:7** But even the very hairs of your head are all numbered. Fear not therefore: ye are of more value than many sparrows.

Think of a little child in a family that is abusive or oppressive. It may be difficult for a child to escape from. I pray for little children in such situations. If they have friends, teachers or grandparents that they could tell what is happening, perhaps there could be a place of refuge for the child. God can provide avenues of help and deliverance. I know when they are in the formative years of brain development and things are very traumatic at home, the detriments to that child could be lifelong. Any parent may be able to make some wise decisions to protect the children and themselves from situations that can lead to mental and physical health conditions.

I use the word abuse very boldly. Abuse can be physical, emotional and oppressive. Oppression destroys a person's soul, it seems. When you live in a family with a person who is trying to punish or make you something less than you are, this damages the spirit to the point one can believe you are not worthy to take your place as who God created you to be. I think in a religious oppression you come to believe that even God wants you to lay yourself out as the dirt for all to tread upon. I don't think God wants us to be like the ground, but rather, a child of the King.

> **Isaiah 51:22-23** Thus saith thy Lord the LORD, and thy God *that* pleadeth the cause of his people, Behold, I have taken out of thine hand the cup of trembling, *even* the dregs of the cup of my fury; thou shalt no more drink it again: But I will put it into the hand of them that afflict thee; which have said to thy soul, Bow down, that we may go over: and thou hast laid thy body as the ground, and as the street, to them that went over. Awake, awake; put on thy strength, O Zion; put on thy beautiful garments, O Jerusalem, the holy city: for henceforth there shall no more come into thee the uncircumcised and the unclean. Shake thyself from the dust; arise, *and* sit down, O Jerusalem: loose thyself from the bands of thy neck, O captive daughter of Zion. For thus saith the LORD, Ye have sold yourselves for nought; and ye shall be redeemed without money. For thus saith the Lord GOD, My people went down aforetime into Egypt to sojourn there; and the Assyrian oppressed them without cause. Now therefore, what have I here, saith the LORD, that my people is taken away for nought? they that rule over them make them to howl, saith the LORD; and my name continually every day *is* blasphemed. Therefore my people shall know my name: therefore *they shall know* in that day that I *am* he that doth speak: behold, *it is* I. How beautiful upon

the mountains are the feet of him that bringeth good tidings, that publisheth peace; that bringeth good tidings of good, that publisheth salvation; that saith unto Zion, Thy God reigneth! Thy watchmen shall lift up the voice; with the voice together shall they sing: for they shall see eye to eye, when the LORD shall bring again Zion. Break forth into joy, sing together, ye waste places of Jerusalem: for the LORD hath comforted his people, he hath redeemed Jerusalem.

A bad situation can be changed through prayer. God can change situations and people; He may lead us to avenues that will incorporate change. It could help to be really open with your feelings. Let the other person know how it feels to you when they treat you in these ways of oppression and abuse. Sometimes the other person is not open to talk, and it may be a situation intentionally meant to eliminate you. When I was in the violent relationship with my first son's father, I did not talk to anyone and did not trust anyone else to make my decisions for me. So I kept on trying to save this man from destruction, to the point that I was the one who was destroyed. And what was happening to my son was so devastating there are no words to describe. We are more educated today than in those years. I lay myself as an example to any parent who finds themselves in such violence and abuse. You may be able to stand up and walk away, and your surface wounds may heal. Even the psychological wounds may heal, but it could take your whole life to accomplish it. Then the children, whose little brains can't process this kind of trauma; may have repercussions that could be with them for life. I think it would have been better if I had of talked to someone about what was happening to me: a doctor or social worker; if nothing else, a police officer. I was not a Christian at that time of my life or I would have never been in that relationship. Ultimately Jesus is the answer to these situations. If we find Him in the midst of the storm and look to Him to pull us out of the fire, He will: have faith. Remember He is the one who saves, not you.

29.

HE LOVES EVEN THE SPARROWS

*I*f you come out of a bad relationship, whether with a spouse, a religious cult, or any number of things, let God teach you the value of who He created you to be. Do not let men rob you of your value, both to the world around you, especially to God and, of course to yourself. It was taught in the religious group that I was in, that to be proud of one's self, was sinful. Don't get me wrong, pride is a sin but let's separate pride from every day self confidence. This thought of pride was taken so far that the practice was of a self-imposed humility. When you would ask a question, it was most often answered in the negative as if the answer was not known, or was in question lest the giver appear proud or positive. This very thought induces your mind to have no will. This is what destroys a person's spirit, so to speak. You think so little of yourself that you let people take advantage of you and walk on you. You allow others to make your decisions even when you are quite capable of making decisions on your own with God's leading. The teaching of this group was that you should not have a will and if you displayed your own will you could be brought into the scrutiny of the church, and asked to repent. When you are brainwashed you really believe that God wants you to be without a mind of your own, and that you should do whatever men tell you to do. We know the Bible teaches against being proud, but there is a healthy state of mind, that we can have a confidence and we do not feel obligated to put ourselves down. A healthy mind can admit when you are wrong, and it is okay. God gives us a will to live and to do His good pleasure. Our will should be subject to His will. But to believe that we are subject to the will of men, can become very destructive to our soul. In making ourselves vulnerable in this way, we are prime targets to be overpowered by other people. We can lose sight of God and fear men instead. God made us with a will to choose to follow Him. When we are His, we love Him and His ways are pleasantness to us. He does not force us to follow Him. We follow because we love Him. There is a peace inside when we walk with God. When you are under the control of men, and your will is dead, it can be mistaken for peace because you have no opinion of your own. You become a mindless puppet. God did not create us to be puppets.

> **Philippians 2:13** For it is God which worketh in you both to will and to do of *his* good pleasure.

> **Hebrews 13:20-21** Now the God of peace, that brought again from the dead our Lord Jesus, that great shepherd of the sheep, through the blood of the everlasting covenant, Make you perfect in every good work to do his will, working in you that which is wellpleasing in his sight, through Jesus Christ; to whom *be* glory for ever and ever. Amen.

When I received an inheritance from my mother, it was a fair sum of money. I had plans to spend it wisely as I would probably never have another large sum of money in my lifetime. I wanted to build a garage and get a storage shed which I hoped to make into a workshop. I needed to drill a deep well, as my shallow well was extremely limited when it came to watering the garden. Watering a lawn was not even a consideration. I also wanted to invest in something that would bring back an increase over some years. When I discussed these issues with the deacon, he called several men's meetings. They made all my decisions for me and told me I should not do any of these things, that I should just spend it on daily living. This goes so against my grain, but I did what they said because I thought they were the authority; until I had nothing left. Soon my well went dry during a drought and I had to take out a bank loan to drill a deep well; the expense has been a huge hardship. Then I was blind and brainwashed, now I can see because God delivered me of the fear and deception. Their system of control and manipulation over people's lives just does not work unless fear is alive. This incident is what taught me that I can be confident, with Jesus I can journey through this life and make responsible decisions and benefit from doing so.

> **Matthew 10:29-31** Are not two sparrows sold for a farthing? and one of them shall not fall on the ground without your Father. But the very hairs of your head are all numbered. Fear ye not therefore, ye are of more value than many sparrows. This has always been a scripture that Jesus comforts me with. He cares and I am His little child. He loves me.

> **Isaiah 10:1-2** Woe unto them that decree unrighteous decrees, and that write grievousness *which* they have prescribed; To turn aside the needy from judgment, and to take away the right from the poor of my people, that widows may be their prey, and *that* they may rob the fatherless!

There are times when He makes our faces like flint, He has to so we can arise and climb out of the dunghill. When I came out of the Mennonites they wanted to save me from hell. I wasn't going there and I knew it. My health was so bad I could not take any more abuse. At night my heart would occasionally become so weak that it was like I was in a state of suspended animation. I did not know if I would live or die. My Lord is so precious, He let me know He was right there; He filled my bedroom with a soft light. I was so amazed I looked to see where the light might be coming from. There were no shadows, it filled every corner and on all sides of my bed. I just rested to know He was there whether I lived or died. It was a feeling of softness and no fear.

I knew that I simply could not take any more blows to my health. I had to put up strong boundaries and let them know they were not welcome to cross them. God made me strong. In the Mennonites teachings, to be strong like that was sin, Satan was always accusing me. But God countered him with scripture and told me that He was the One making me that way. I often questioned this strength before my Lord and He gave me such reassurance of what He was doing and that He had to make me strong for the work. He was lifting me up out of the dunghill. This was His Word to me.

> **Ezekiel 2:6-8** And thou, son of man, be not afraid of them, neither be afraid of their words, though briers and thorns *be* with thee, and thou dost dwell among scorpions: be not afraid of their words, nor be dismayed at their looks, though they *be* a rebellious house. And thou shalt speak my words unto them, whether they will hear, or whether they will forbear: for they *are* most rebellious. But thou, son of man, hear what I say unto thee; Be not thou rebellious like that rebellious house: open thy mouth, and eat that I give thee.

Ezekiel 3:8-11 Behold, I have made thy face strong against their faces, and thy forehead strong against their foreheads. As an adamant harder than flint have I made thy forehead: fear them not, neither be dismayed at their looks, though they *be* a rebellious house. Moreover he said unto me, Son of man, all my words that I shall speak unto thee receive in thine heart, and hear with thine ears. And go, get thee to them of the captivity, unto the children of thy people, and speak unto them, and tell them, Thus saith the Lord GOD; whether they will hear, or whether they will forbear.

Isaiah 50:7-8 For the Lord GOD will help me; therefore shall I not be confounded: therefore have I set my face like a flint, and I know that I shall not be ashamed. *He is* near that justifieth me; who will contend with me? let us stand together: who *is* mine adversary? let him come near to me.

Micah 4:11-13 Now also many nations are gathered against thee, that say, Let her be defiled, and let our eye look upon Zion. But they know not the thoughts of the LORD, neither understand they his counsel: for he shall gather them as the sheaves into the floor. Arise and thresh, O daughter of Zion: for I will make thine horn iron, and I will make thy hoofs brass: and thou shalt beat in pieces many people: and I will consecrate their gain unto the LORD, and their substance unto the Lord of the whole earth.

Isaiah 8:11-13 For the LORD spake thus to me with a strong hand, and instructed me that I should not walk in the way of this people, saying, Say ye not, A confederacy, to all *them to* whom this people shall say, A confederacy; neither fear ye their fear, nor be afraid. Sanctify the LORD of hosts himself; and *let* him *be* your fear, and *let* him *be* your dread.

Isaiah 44:8 Fear ye not, neither be afraid: have not I told thee from that time, and have declared *it*? ye *are* even my witnesses. Is there a God beside me? yea, *there is* no God; I know not *any*.

Joshua 1:9 Have not I commanded thee? Be strong and of a good courage; be not afraid, neither be thou dismayed: for the LORD thy God *is* with thee whithersoever thou goest.

30.

WE CAN OVERCOME

*I*n spite of this strength that God gave me, I had to find a way out of the anger that rose up in me when I thought of my diminished health, finances, and the many afflictions I bore through that were so absurd. If only this strength would have come earlier, then I would not have allowed them to take advantage of me. But the bottom line was that I had to be delivered of the fear first so I could see Jesus, and so I could be delivered of the man-made doctrines: the fear of these men whom I believed were God's messengers. There is such a brain-washing that takes place. Only God Himself can "un-wash" the brain. And when I cried out to Him, He heard me. He came to me and what He did to heal my mind was so of Him and not of man, it was beyond human.

> **Exodus 22:22-24** Ye shall not afflict any widow, or fatherless child. If thou afflict them in any wise, and they cry at all unto me, I will surely hear their cry; And my wrath shall wax hot, and I will kill you with the sword; and your wives shall be widows, and your children fatherless.

Sometimes I was not sure who was the maddest-me or God, or whether it was okay for me to be mad because He was mad. I did not talk about all the incidents while I was among them. Once again I held it all in except to talk to a few very close friends. I thought this was the noble thing to do so as not to bring accusation or a bad name to these leaders. But as I had left their midst, and especially after one church man, with his wife, showed up here, when the gate had been left open for the UPS man, I then spoke of a few of the incidents. This man said, "These things ought not to be". Indeed my sentiments as well. He also conveyed to me that it was common knowledge that they intended to move me into town. No one had told me about this or I would have told them to go fly a kite. I, putting it all together, assumed this was the reason I was not encouraged to spend any of my money to upgrade my homestead.

So the Lord began to prompt me to open Pandora's Box and let out these things that had been done. I wrote letters first to the offenders and spelled it out, all that they had done behind my back and to my face, and then with other choice ones in whom the Lord directed me. I never got any response, but I continue to pray for the offenders and for the group as a whole, and the lives that are still held captive under their manipulation, control and false doctrine.

Oh, we are in the last days and we must be watchful of deceivers. Read God's Holy Word day in and day out, be prayerful and full of faith. And where we fall down, we need to look to our merciful Lord to pick us up and heal our wounds with His holy ointment. Be patient and kind with yourself. Ask the Lord to help you see yourself the way He sees you.

If we do sin in these circumstances, let us repent and come to our Savior for forgiveness. And if our enemies repent of their transgressions, may we forgive them as Christ has forgiven us. Let not your heart be hardened. We are all sinners trudging this roughed path with the hope of salvation in the end. It has helped me to earnestly pray for my persecutors and ask God to give me unconditional love for them. This kind of love is of God, not of men. Beg Him for it. He said He would not give us a stone if we ask Him for bread.

> **Luke 23:34** Then said Jesus, Father, forgive them; for they know not what they do. And they parted his raiment, and cast lots.

> **Matthew 5:44-45** But I say unto you, Love your enemies, bless them that curse you, do good to them that hate you, and pray for them which despitefully use you, and persecute you; That ye may be the children of your Father which is in heaven: for he maketh his sun to rise on the evil and on the good, and sendeth rain on the just and on the unjust.

> **Luke 11:1-13** And it came to pass, that, as he was praying in a certain place, when he ceased, one of his disciples said unto him, Lord, teach us to pray, as John also taught his disciples. And he said unto them, When ye pray, say, Our Father which art in heaven, Hallowed be thy name. Thy kingdom come. Thy will be done, as in heaven, so in earth. Give us day by day our daily bread. And forgive us our sins; for we also forgive every one that is indebted to us. And lead us not into temptation; but deliver us from evil. And he said unto them, Which of you shall have a friend, and shall go unto him at midnight, and say unto him, Friend, lend me three loaves; For a friend of mine in his journey is come to me, and I have nothing to set before him? And he from within shall answer and say, Trouble me not: the door is now shut, and my children are with me in bed; I cannot rise and give thee. I say unto you, Though he will not rise and give him, because he is his friend, yet because of his importunity he will rise and give him

as many as he needeth. And I say unto you, Ask, and it shall be given you; seek, and ye shall find; knock, and it shall be opened unto you. For every one that asketh receiveth; and he that seeketh findeth; and to him that knocketh it shall be opened. If a son shall ask bread of any of you that is a father, will he give him a stone? or if *he ask* a fish, will he for a fish give him a serpent? Or if he shall ask an egg, will he offer him a scorpion? If ye then, being evil, know how to give good gifts unto your children: how much more shall *your* heavenly Father give the Holy Spirit to them that ask him?

Let us pray and worship our God, fore He only is worthy. Amen.

31.

THE PAINTING

I will conclude my writings with an explanation of the book cover. It was a vision from God at the time I came out of the Mennonites. Others also had come out before me and not long following, one of which passed on into eternity. The vision portrays people in various degrees of bondage and deliverance. The swan on the left is very leery and is partially satisfied to stay where he is because there is a little light in his bondage. The cattails portray confinement. The swan in the forefront has made his decision to break lose but is held down by oppression. The man is the oppressor. The Lord showed me as the painting unfolded that the fighting swan is trapped in dark waters and the oppression comes from with-out of the heart, reaching in; the battle is fierce. The two swans on the right have escaped and are set free, swimming away and in the Light, but still in this world. The swan in the far distance has escaped the bondage and has crossed over into eternity, forever to dwell in the Light of God. The swans are specifically Trumpeter Swans portraying the call to sound the trumpet of truth that others too may be set free.

Isaiah 61:1-3 The Spirit of the Lord GOD *is* upon me; because the LORD hath anointed me to preach good tidings unto the meek; he hath sent me to bind up the brokenhearted, to proclaim liberty to the captives, and the opening of the prison to *them that are* bound; To proclaim the acceptable year of the LORD, and the day of vengeance of our God; to comfort all that mourn; To appoint unto them that mourn in Zion, to give unto them beauty for ashes, the oil of joy for mourning, the garment of praise for the spirit of heaviness; that they might be called trees of righteousness, the planting of the LORD, that he might be glorified.

May God bless each heart with strength, truth and His Holy Spirit.
THE END

Epilogue

Now being delivered of fear, my body can rest from the "fight and flight" engagement. This gives my adrenal glands a rest and the opportunity to rejuvenate. With time I have gained some strength and vigor. I am no longer like a woman teetering on the edge of death.

God changed my prison garments and I, with glee, pulled on blue jeans and my boots and relaxed in my new life outside of prison walls.

> **Jeremiah 52:33** And changed his prison garments: and he did continually eat bread before him all the days of his life.

But after twenty two years of life in the Mennonites, wearing a certain type of dress and a black kerchief on my bound up hair; it was a step of courage to go down town in jeans for the first time. I felt free before God, but most everyone I knew in town only knew me as a Mennonite. I prayed for courage and set out on this new adventure. And the encounters that I received were so uplifting, people that saw me regularly would make remarks such as, "You look so good, your face has color!" Well I took that, as that my face before, was ghostly looking. Others would say, "Your face looks so good, the stress is gone". Some said I looked like I was getting younger instead of older. I had let my hair down and people commented on my beautiful long hair. These were people like the gas station attendant or the cashier at the grocery store, and my neighbors. For months God protected me from encounters with Mennonites, until I was confident enough that it did not cause me stress to visit with them in my blue jeans and my flowing hair. The remarks from people in town continue even still today, three years later. I thank folks for their remarks and tell them that it helps build up my confidence that I am healing, getting stronger and simply set free.

I want to encourage every reader to put your faith in the Lord Jesus Christ. Bring to the cross, all your sins, believing in the Messiah to wash you and make you clean and worthy, by His blood, to stand before the Father. We are in the very last years on earth. I feel we are standing on the threshold of the Great Tribulation. It is my personal belief that the rapture of the saints, (all the saved) will precede the Tribulation. I hope to encourage everyone who has not yet given up their sinful life to follow Jesus, to make it your earnest endeavor. Time is short and none of us want to be left here on earth to endure the "wrath of God" during the tribulation. But if you are left behind and you are a father or a mother, and your children were taken up; my heart breaks even now to think of your sorrow. Please take heart and know that they are safe in the arms of Jesus and they are beyond sorrow and pain. They will be forever with God. I pray for you, even now, that you will make your choice, it is not too late; to worship God and accept the sacrifice He has made to save your soul from eternal damnation. Seek Him and you shall find Him, love Him with all your heart and soul.

> **Revelation 14:19** And the angel thrust in his sickle into the earth, and gathered the vine of the earth, and cast *it* into the great winepress of the wrath of God.

Epilogue

Revelation 19:15 And out of his mouth goeth a sharp sword, that with it he should smite the nations: and he shall rule them with a rod of iron: and he treadeth the winepress of the fierceness and wrath of Almighty God.

I had a dream on Passover at the time of the fullness of the "blood red moon", April 4, 2015.

The dream:

The phone rang and I picked it up in my bedroom, it was my son, Jim's voice, he said, "This is it". I said, "What?" Then he repeated, "This is it!" And right then in a "twinkling of an eye" I went up in the "rapture".

I felt the power that lifted me up through the ceiling of my room, delivering my body into the ethers; there are no words to describe that power. It happened in a twinkling of an eye, indeed. I heard an explanation of how much "time" is a twinkling of an eye and it is a split second, for sure, something akin to the speed of light.

This dream woke me with a start and I was actually surprised to find that I was still in this world. This happened exactly on the blood red moon on Passover. The Bible teaches that there will be signs in the heavens that will warn us of His coming, and blood red moons are mentioned. We had four in a period of two years and each one fell on a Biblical feast day. This is phenomenal and I hope that these events have brought you to a state of watchfulness. Jesus wants everyone to be saved. The events that will unfold in the Tribulation will not come unannounced. His Word gives us warning, the heavens and the earth are crying out to us to listen to the voice of God.

When I arose from my bed I went out to view the blood red moon. I had not known at what hour it would happen so I did not set an alarm clock. But at the stage I saw the moon, all but a sliver, was red. It was surely perfectly red at the moment of my dream. This was no doubt a message that God was giving me: the signs in the sky and His coming to reap the saints.

> **1 Corinthians 15:52** In a moment, in the twinkling of an eye, at the last trump: for the trumpet shall sound, and the dead shall be raised incorruptible, and we shall be changed.

> **1 Thessalonians 4:16-18** For the Lord himself shall descend from heaven with a shout, with the voice of the archangel, and with the trump of God: and the dead in Christ shall rise first: Then we which are alive *and* remain shall be caught up together with them in the clouds, to meet the Lord in the air: and so shall we ever be with the Lord. Wherefore comfort one another with these words.

> **Acts 2:19-21** And I will shew wonders in heaven above, and signs in the earth beneath; blood, and fire, and vapour of smoke: The sun shall be turned into darkness, and the moon into blood, before that great and notable day of the Lord come: And it shall come to pass, *that* whosoever shall call on the name of the Lord shall be saved.

> **Revelation 6:12** And I beheld when he had opened the sixth seal, and, lo, there was a great earthquake; and the sun became black as sackcloth of hair, and the moon became as blood;

> **Matthew 24:42** Watch therefore: for ye know not what hour your Lord doth come.

With prayers my friend, go with God.

CPSIA information can be obtained
at www.ICGtesting.com
Printed in the USA
FSHW012233180619
59203FS